UNCHOSEN PRESIDENTS

Allan P. Sindler

Unchosen Presidents

The Vice-President and Other

Frustrations of Presidential Succession

University of California Press
Berkeley • Los Angeles • London

University of California Press
Berkeley and Los Angeles, California

University of California Press, Ltd.
London, England

ISBN 0-520-03185-7
Library of Congress Catalog Card Number: 75-46041
Printed in the United States of America

For my mother
A teacher by example

Contents

Acknowledgments

This study provides a nice example of the mutual stimulation of teaching and research. Several years ago, when teaching an undergraduate class dealing with diverse policy problems, I found myself dissatisfied with my capacity to respond to questions about the persistent mediocrity of vice-presidents and in my reliance on ad hoc rejection of one or another reform on that subject proposed by members of the class. That dissatisfaction led me to begin to develop an analytic frame for the problem, initially reported on in "Completing a Presidential Term with a Successor of Presidential Caliber" (*Policy Studies Journal,* summer 1974), and ultimately it led to the writing of this book. At all stages of the inquiry I profited from student commentary on the problem, in turn fueled by the unprecedented set of resignations and successions surrounding the presidency and vice-presidency in 1973-1974. I learned much from "teaching the problem" to and with students, and I am appreciative to them for probing and pushing as hard as they did.

Several colleagues reviewed an earlier draft and provided helpful suggestions for improvement: Barbara Hinckley, Arnold Meltsner, Nelson Polsby, Austin Ranney, and Aaron Wildavsky. Two unknown colleagues, in their role as external evaluators for the University of California Press, also added useful points for strengthening the study. The analysis presented here is the better because of their comments, for which I am grateful.

1

Setting the Problem

Even in the self-lacerating America of the late 1960s a prediction that someday soon the elected president and vice-president would resign and that an appointed vice-president would become the new president would have rung hollow. And yet it all came to happen in the short period from late 1973 through midsummer 1974.

Foolproof assurance of persistent probity by incumbents in high governmental office cannot be had, of course, by institutional design. Hence even as we deplore the individual betrayals of public trust that led to the forced resignations of Spiro Agnew and Richard Nixon and even as we subsequently explore ways to alter the governmental process to make recurrence of such behavior unlikely, we know that it is the personal qualities of the incumbent which are ultimately controlling. How we provide for presidential succession, however, is at bottom a question of institutional design open to our determination and control. Because our current arrangements have produced a nonelected president and vice-president, the timeliness of reengaging the old and vexing problem of presidential succession in America needs no belaboring. That problem is the focus of this study.

Unanticipated Use of the Twenty-fifth Amendment

It is ironic but instructive to note that the path to succession following the coerced resignations of Agnew and Nixon was set by the terms of a carefully considered and recently adopted solution to a different problem, also old and vexing, namely that of presidential disability. It bears reminding, especially at the outset of an inquiry concentrating on institutional process, that even the most thoughtful policy response to a problem is likely to be later applied in unanticipated situations and to produce unintended consequences. When the basic design of government constitutes the problem area—as in the present focus on presidential succession—the fallibility of knowledge and the unpredictability of events often will cause today's solution to reemerge as one of tomorrow's pressing problems.

Two provisions of the Twenty-fifth Amendment, adopted in 1967, came to determine succession in 1973-1974 in a context different from the question of presidential disablity, which was the principal concern of the measure. Section 1 called for the vice-president to succeed to a vacated presidency and ruled out use of a special presidential election. Section 2 set a new policy of filling a

vacancy in the vice-presidency and chose appointment as the mode:

Whenever there is a vacancy in the office of the Vice-
President, the President shall nominate a Vice-President
who shall take office upon confirmation by a majority
vote of both houses of Congress.

When the Twenty-fifth Amendment was under
consideration, sections 1 and 2 occasioned little
legislative or public discussion compared to the
attention given the provisions on presidential disability. Yet it was these first two sections, and not
the heart of the amendment, that came into play
first in 1973 and again in 1974, and that led to
America's government being headed by appointees. President Gerald Ford was initially appointed
vice-president after the resignation of Spiro Agnew
in late 1973, and he succeeded to the presidency in
August 1974 upon Richard Nixon's resignation.
The process then continued in conformity with
section 2: in the latter half of 1974 Nelson Rockefeller was nominated to the vice-presidency by
President Ford and confirmed by Congress.

Anyone caring to apply the unerring wisdom of
post-1974 hindsight could easily fault the promo-
ters of the Twenty-fifth Amendment. They appar-
ently failed either to realize or, at the least, to act
on the realization that sections 1 and 2, under the
right combination of circumstances, would make
inevitable the simultaneous incumbency of an appointed president and vice-president. But what was
a reasonable mid-sixties view of the chances that

such circumstances would occur? A look backward
revealed, after all, that a double vacancy had never
occurred in our history.[1] Every time the presidency
had become prematurely vacant, an elected vice-
president was in office and succeeded to the presidency. Every time the vice-presidency had become
prematurely vacant and remained unfilled, the
elected president completed his term of office
without need for successorship. And no look forward—not even one offered as a hypothetical, far-
out "horror story"—could have been expected to
foretell the bizarre developments that led to the
resignations of Agnew and Nixon for unrelated
gross betrayals of public trust and office. The
occurrence of two such unprecedented events within
a year and in the same administration remains
difficult to accept and comprehend, even in retrospect. It would be foolish, therefore, to tax 1967's
leadership for having overlooked the possibility of

---

[1] My use of several terms should be clarified at the outset.
"Direct" or "immediate" successorship refers to the initially
selected vice-president, whether elected or appointed, who is
the first to succeed to a vacated presidency. "Double vacancy"
refers to a situation in which the presidency is vacated prior
to the expiration of the term of office by the originally elected
president, and at a time when the original vice-president who
came in with him has earlier left office without completing
his term. "Contingent" successorship refers to the line of
succession which comes into play in situations of a double
vacancy. It includes all persons designated by Congress to
succeed to the presidency in the event the initially selected
vice-president is unable to do so, including anyone appointed
to fill a vacancy in the vice-presidency.

such happenings and how the Twenty-fifth Amendment would affect them.[2]

LIMITED AND CONFUSED REACTION

Of greater profit and pertinence is an inquiry into our own limited reactions now that the unexpected has indeed occurred and a nation with pride in its democracy finds itself in the anomalous position of being governed by appointed national leaders. Predictably, there has been an upsurge of concern about the wisdom of sections 1 and 2 and, more generally, about the fundamentals of presidential succession. But, contrary to what might be anticipated, that concern to date falls far short of a groundswell. There are few stirrings on behalf of basic reform, much less any emerging crisis of legitimacy. That President Ford and Vice-President Rockefeller were not elected, that each owed his office to his predecessor, and that each had more than half a term to serve appear to bother some commentators more than the public. The uniqueness of the precipitating events doubtless has inhibited the growth of more widespread and intense adverse reaction. A double vacancy caused by the resignations of the elected incumbents has

[2] The same reasoning justifies Congress's predominant concern with presidential disability. The historical record contained not only the older instances of disabled presidents (Garfield and Wilson) but also the very recent examples of illness of Eisenhower and Johnson. Statistically, the probability of the occurrence of presidential disability is obviously much higher than that of a double vacancy.

been discounted by many as an historical fluke, a million-to-one improbability not likely to recur. Then, too, the public's relief at having the extended and agonizing Watergate period brought to a close has carried over to acceptance of Ford's succession to the White House. Hence even most of those dissatisfied with some aspect of successorship arrangements as they worked out this time have little disposition to reopen the issue or to push for alteration of sections 1 and 2.

And those who have been persuaded by the events of 1973 and 1974 to call for revamping the succession process diverge greatly in their assessments. They approach a common outlook only in opposing retention of sections 1 and 2 in their present form. Otherwise, their prescriptions for change vary enormously, reflecting different problem definitions, conceptions, and philosophies. A strengthening of the vice-presidency is urged by some, whereas others insist the office should be abolished. Some push for a sharper separation of the vice-president from the president, others for the reverse. Some would repeal section 2 of the Twenty-fifth Amendment, but others would mandate it as the way to select all vice-presidents. Overall, there has been little joining of issues and much obfuscation of areas of agreement and disagreement, and on what bases.

In sum, I write this essay on presidential succession in an early period of reaction to recent events. Thus far there is neither an aroused public opinion clamoring for change nor is there among the minority of leaders and commentators pushing for change any consensus on what to substitute for present arrangements. This condition reflects in part the numbing novelty of the events, which presumably is remediable by the mere passage of time. It also reflects, however, relative analytic neglect of the subject of presidential succession, a deficiency which initially stimulated the inquiry undertaken in this book and which sets its purposes and approach.

Purposes and Approach of This Study

Unlike most of the writing on this subject, this study is not an advocacy piece organized around or culminating in a defense of a single prescription for change preferred by the author. Its central purpose, rather, is to systematically, analytically, and broadly examine the long-time, frustrating problem of the vice-presidency and presidential succession. My chief concerns, accordingly, have been to develop an analytic frame in an effort not only to impose greater order and clarity on the diverse range of arguments and proposals, but to enable the reader (and the policy maker) to choose among alternative feasible solutions with a more explicit understanding of their relative strengths and weaknesses. The clarification of feasible choices on presidential succession devices, measured against the dynamics of our political system, lies at the heart of the analytic objective I have set for this essay. To the degree this objective is met, the reader should be able to come to an informed judgment on which solution he might prefer and—no less importantly—why.

FORMULATING THE PROBLEM

Typically, the problem of presidential succession is linked to the vice-presidency and then cast in something like the following form: *how can we assure that vice-presidents will be selected with primary reference to their successorship role?, that is, a routine and regular provision of vice-presidents who are seen to be, at the time of their selection, of presumed presidential quality.* This view of the problem can be reformulated generically, without being limited to the vice-presidency: *how can we assure that an uncompleted presidential term will be completed by a successor of presumed presidential quality?* Both statements of the problem may be handled, as will be seen, by use of the same analytic themes. I develop these themes initially in an extensive treatment of the first problem formulation focusing on the vice-presidency and then extend them in a brief and complementary consideration of the second, more general, formulation.

The concept of "a routine and regular selection of persons of presumed presidential quality" cannot escape being somewhat ambiguous and slippery, but its meaning for purposes of this analysis can be made clear enough. It should not be misread as implying that we know or can measure the attributes of "high presidential quality." Clearly, we lack such knowledge. Hence it should also not be taken as suggesting that if we drew presidential successors only from among those who had certain political career lines or who were incumbents in certain public offices, we would thereby guarantee that the successor would in fact make a very good president. My use of the concept is more modest and involves two factors: the political status and repute of the person selected for the presidential successorship post and the intent behind the selection.

Persons of *presumed presidential quality* would ordinarily be those who, at the time of their selection as vice-presidential nominee, enjoyed significant and positive national standing and recognition. Typically, they would currently hold or would have recently held important, visible office; in either case their conduct of that office would have given them favorable prominence. Often, though not invariably, they would have competed for a presidential nomination and shown some solid popular and party appeal. The factor of *intent* can be gauged by determining whether vice-presidential nominees are chosen primarily for their presidential successorship role. (The same measure of intent can be applied to those in contingent successor posts, such as the Speaker of the House, who would become president in the event the vice-presidency was unfilled and the presidency became vacant.)

When a relatively minor or obscure official is designated for the vice-presidential post, little concern for presidential-quality successorship may be inferred—for example, Representative William E. Miller, Republican, 1964; Governor Spiro Agnew, Republican, 1968; Senator Thomas Eagleton (withdrew) and Sargent Shriver, Democrats, 1972. The opposite situation, however, does not by itself demonstrate a positive intent to seek out high-quality presidential succession, because a prestigious running-mate may be selected primarily to satisfy other purposes—Johnson under Kennedy, Democrat, 1960, and Humphrey under Johnson, Democrat, 1964. To be sure, the selection of a prominent leader as the vice-presidential nominee fully meets the standard of presidential-quality succession, regardless of intent. But it is reasonable to suppose that the provision of high-quality successorship on a *routine, regular basis* can come about only as a result of a procedure, practice, or tradition that explicitly seeks to achieve that objective, whatever other purposes it may also serve.

Another way to formulate the problem shifts attention from the quality desired of the successor to the characteristics desired of the succession process. Presidential succession, in this view, should be seen as *the need to provide a rapid and stable process which will produce a successor considered legitimate and acceptable by the public.* Whether satisfaction of this need is held to complement or conflict with the need for presidential-quality successorship constitutes a critical turning point in the analysis undertaken in this study. It should also be noted that in this problem definition, as in the previous one, the vice-presidency is assigned no monopolistic position and is treated as but one of several alternative solutions warranting examination. Indeed, whether the vice-presidency should be retained at all is handled as an open question suitable for review.

2

The Framers, the Constitution, and the Congress on the Vice-Presidency and Succession

Taken by itself, the vice-presidency has always been a most anomalous office. The sole constitutional power of its incumbent, while the presidency is filled, is to preside over the Senate and to exercise a vote in that body in case of a tie. Yet the vice-president has been assigned the enormously important role of presidential successorship. How, then, does one attract to the vice-presidency—an office little better than "nothing" but which could suddenly become "everything"—persons of presumed presidential quality? A careful look at what the Framers tried by way of an answer provides a useful starting point for the inquiry. The objective, of course, is neither to sanctify nor repudiate past authority but simply to learn what we can from the efforts of others who have had to come to grips with this vexing problem.

The Framers' Abortive
Vice-Presidential Solution

The Framers' logically compelling solution derived from the common-sense expectation that persons thought to be of presidential caliber would contest for the presidency, but not for the vice-presidency. Why not provide, then, solely for a presidential election and simply designate the presidential runner-up as vice-president? With each elector authorized to cast a vote for each of two candidates, the success of the Framers' solution depended on the willingness of electors to confine their votes to genuine presidential candidates. If the persons for whom votes were cast were informally differentiated as to presidential and vice-presidential positions, the objective would be thoroughly undercut. The vice-presidency would then be won by the leading vice-presidential contestant, not by the major losing presidential contender.

Implicit in the Framers' solution was a conception of government in which parties either did not exist or were content to have the presidency occupied by a leader of one party and the vice-presidency by a leader of another party. When that conception proved unrealistic, the solution aborted. Parties rapidly emerged—their beginnings were evident during George Washington's tenure—and they brought in their wake an insistence on distinguishing between presidential and vice-presidential aspirants. Once that discrimination occurred, the

assignment of the vice-presidency to the major
defeated presidential candidate was no longer considered appropriate or desirable; the winning presidential party wanted to control the vice-presidency
as well.

After the repudiation of the premise underlying
the Framers' solution, the election procedure
proved so defective with respect to safeguarding
presidential choice that formal amendment of the
Constitution became a necessity. If the electors of
the dominant party, for example, supported its
presidential and vice-presidential entrants equally,
the choice between them—as occurred in 1800,
with Jefferson and Burr—would be thrown into the
lame-duck House of Representatives, with both
technically having an identical claim to the presidency. To prevent such an outcome the dominant
party could deliberately give its vice-presidential
candidate a few less electoral votes than its presidential candidate, but the losing party's presidential aspirant might then capture the vice-presidency
—as in 1796, with Jefferson beating out Adams's
running mate, Pinckney.

The minority party, for its part, was not merely
the passive beneficiary of strategic miscalculations
by the dominant party but also had its own lever-
age to exercise. It could in effect demand control of
the vice-presidential post by threatening otherwise
to have its electors cast enough votes for the
dominant party's vice-presidential candidate to enable him to secure the most electoral votes and
hence to become president. This strategy was

seriously considered by the Federalist party before the 1804 election, demonstrating the vulnerability of the election procedures to forms of exploitation never anticipated by the Framers. If such a "blackmail" threat were carried out successfully, it would assuredly result in a vice-president of presidential caliber—but at the intolerable cost of producing a president of vice-presidential quality! The dominant party could do little but accede to the threat, in effect protecting its right to have its presidential candidate win the presidency by conceding the vice-presidential office to the opposition. Such a result would conform to the Framers' intent with respect to the vice-presidency, but it was no longer a tolerable outcome in an age of party rivalry.

With grave deficiencies in the election process made starkly evident in 1796 and 1800, and with further manipulation in the prospect for 1804, the corrective Twelfth Amendment was pushed through before the 1804 election. Formally it constituted a watershed for the vice-presidency, though it but recognized officially what had transpired already in the de facto redefinition of the path to the office and of the character of its incumbent. It guaranteed that the presidency would be won by a presidential and not a vice-presidential candidate, but at the price of establishing a separate vice-presidential race and thereby discouraging competition by presidential-quality persons for the post. By pairing the presidential and vice-presidential candidates as a team to be voted on together and not separately, it assured same-party outcomes but at the cost of the vice-president's thorough subordination to the president. In sum, the Twelfth Amendment formally set the stage for the problems that have beset the vice-presidency and presidential succession to our day.

The provision of two votes per elector, which was eliminated by the Twelfth Amendment, exacerbated but did not cause the failings of the Framers' plan.[3] Its fatal flaw was that it required maintenance of a depoliticized environment to sustain presidential contests among "statesmen" unconnected with durable factions. When such political groupings speedily evolved, however, the Framers' rules of the game underwent sudden change. Whereas the Framers' intentions called for the running of presidential candidates only, without distinguishing between presidential and vice-presidential aspirants, the fledgling parties moved at once to structure the choice of candidates for the nation's two highest offices. Even more critically, the substantive premise of the Framers' plan was

[3] The dual vote by electors required that at least one of the votes be cast for a candidate not a resident of the elector's state. As each of the two votes counted equally, and the elector could not indicate any preference between the two candidates voted for, the major purpose of the dual vote provision was to promote nationally known leaders, rather than parochial leaders of populous states, as presidential winners. An incidental benefit of the arrangement was to assure vice-presidents of presidential quality, by assigning that post to the leading presidential loser. See Arthur M. Schlesinger, Jr., "On the Presidential Succession," *Political Science Quarterly*, vol. 89, no. 3 (fall 1974), pp. 488-490.

decisively rejected: having a president and vice-president of different parties was no longer acceptable as the price for securing a vice-president of presidential quality.

The Constitution on Presidential Succession

The original Constitution, in article 2, section 1, required that both the president and the vice-president "be elected," and provided for succession as follows:

> In Case of the Removal of the President from Office, or of his Death, Resignation, or Inability to discharge the Powers and Duties of the said Office, the Same shall devolve on the Vice-President, and the Congress may by Law provide for the Case of Removal, Death, Resignation or Inability, both of the President and Vice-President, declaring what Officer shall then act as President, and such Officer shall act accordingly, until the Disability be removed, or a President shall be elected.

Whether the Framers intended by this language to limit the successorship role of the vice-president is unclear, but later events have placed a different interpretation on the matter and have rendered the issue moot. The language may be read to suggest only a brief provisional successorship role as acting president, pending the outcome of a special presidential election. (If this was the intent, these limitations are all the more impressive in the light of the Framers' design to award the vice-presidency to the runner-up presidential candidate.) The first occasion to apply the provision came with the death of William Henry Harrison shortly after his inauguration in 1841. Amid debate which revealed disagreement and confusion over what the Constitution required, Vice-President John Tyler successfully asserted a right of full successorship for the remainder of the uncompleted term. Successor presidents have held to that practice ever since, and it was explicitly endorsed in the Succession Act of 1947 and section 1 of the Twenty-fifth Amendment.

Whereas successorship to the presidency (whether understood as limited or full) was assigned to the vice-president, the question of successorship to the vice-presidency was left open for Congress to decide, including the possibility of leaving a vacant vice-presidency unfilled. The latter option made the most sense in view of the original award of the vice-presidency to the major losing presidential contestant, for whom there could not be a successor. Lack of a vice-president would raise no serious problems as long as arrangements were made for the handling of a double vacancy. As the quoted paragraph indicates, Congress was empowered to set a succession line in the event of a double vacancy, with the successor serving until "a President shall be elected." This clause, together with the terms of the 1792 act described in the following paragraphs, makes it less open to dispute that the Framers intended to have a short provisional successorship under conditions of a double vacancy. Confirmation of this interpretation by later events cannot be had, of course, because the first occasion of a double vacancy was in 1974, seven years after the Twenty-fifth Amendment had altered the Constitution's original provisions on succession.[4]

The Congress on Presidential Succession

Acting under the authority granted in article 2, section 1, the Second Congress enacted the first presidential succession law in 1792. It provided for the vice-president to succeed to a vacant presidency, but made no provision to fill a vacant vice-presidency. In the event of a double vacancy, the succession line was fixed as the president pro tempore of the Senate or, if none, then the Speaker of the House. If the double vacancy occurred when more than six months of the presidential term remained, the contingent successor would act as president only until a new president was selected by special election.

A few years after the assassination of President Garfield, the Succession Act of 1886 was adopted. It provided for a longer contingency succession list than the 1792 law, and through the Cabinet rather

---

[4] Prior to the passage of the Twenty-fifth Amendment (1967), no successor to Agnew could have been appointed and President Nixon's resignation would then have led to the successorship of Speaker of the House Carl Albert, a Democrat, in 1974. Whether, under those conditions, Nixon would have chosen to resign or the Democratic House would have pressed its impeachment inquiry as it did are matters open to considerable speculation.

than through the top leadership of Congress.[5] Although not explicitly requiring a special election, it
implied that a contingent successor, who would be
tapped only when a double vacancy existed, would
serve as acting president, pending Congress's determination of whether and when to hold a special
presidential election.

The 1947 Succession Act derived from President
Harry Truman's beliefs and particular circumstances. As a successor and not an elected president,
and with nearly a full term to serve, Truman felt
strongly that the president should not be in the
position of being able to name his own successor,
unmediated by an election. With the vice-presidency
vacant, Truman's successor under the terms of the
1886 Act was the secretary of state, a post within his
own appointment authority though subject to
Senate confirmation. Truman also urged that contingent successorship be provisional and that a
special presidential election be held. Congress accepted the first but not the second of his ideas. The
two top legislative leaders were put in ahead of the
Cabinet in the line of contingent succession, this
time with the House Speaker preceding the president pro tempore of the Senate. A special election

---

[5] Too short a contingent succession list may prove risky,
though much depends also on whether the offices designated
are likely to be filled at all times. Thus, in 1881, when
President Garfield was assassinated, neither of the congressional posts specified in the 1792 act was occupied. Had there
not been a vice-president, there would have been no usable
line of succession.

was clearly excluded, with a contingent successor directed to serve "until the expiration of the then current presidential term."

The Twenty-fifth Amendment, adopted in 1967 primarily to deal with presidential disability, also altered the succession process and the place of the vice-president. Together with the Succession Act of 1947, which it leaves intact, it constitutes the presently controlling arrangements on that subject. It provides for the vice-president to become acting president while the president is temporarily disabled or incapacitated, and to assume full successorship as president if the presidency becomes vacant. For the first time, provision is made for filling a vacancy in the vice-presidency—by presidential nomination and congressional confirmation—thus assuring that there will always be a vice-president, except for the period between the date of vacancy and the postconfirmation date of the appointee's assumption of office.

By requiring the filling of a vacant vice-presidency by appointment, the Twenty-fifth Amendment annuls, for such circumstances, the requirement of article 2, section 1 that the vice-president "be elected." Then, by permitting an appointed vice-president to succeed to the presidency in no way different from an elected vice-president, it opens the possibility of annulling the companion requirement of article 2, section 1 that the president "be elected." Further, by empowering such a successor president to appoint a new vice-president subject to congressional confirmation, a cyclical process is authorized without limit on repetition other than the fixed time parameters of a four-year term. President Ford and Vice-President Rockefeller are, of course, the first products of these new arrangements.

Comparing Present to Past Arrangements

Several trends emerge from a comparison of the Twelfth and Twenty-fifth Amendments with the original Constitution and of the 1947 Succession Act with those of 1792 and 1886.

Contingent succession (succession by other than the initial vice-president) has undergone a marked change. What started out as a limited successorship, involving an interim acting president pending the outcome of a special election which would produce a new president, has become a full successorship in authority and for the remainder of the term, without provision for a special election. In its legislation determining the line of contingent succession, Congress has shifted narrowly from top congressional leadership (1792) to the Cabinet in order of rank (1886) and currently to both, with Congress's leaders preceding Cabinet members (1947). The Twenty-fifth Amendment, however, by assuring the filling of a vacant vice-presidency, has made contingent successorship by anyone other than an appointed vice-president statistically improbable. Throughout our history the elected vice-president has been assigned direct successorship to a vacated presidency. Hence once the Twenty-fifth Amendment made an appointed successor vice-president the first contingent successor, presidential succession became locked to the vice-presidency more tightly than ever before.

Another important change concerns the presumed presidential quality of vice-presidents, which was initially assured by the Framers' formula of assigning the post to the runner-up presidential candidate and not having a vice-presidential contest at all. The rapid emergence of party rivalry soon rendered that formula unfeasible. The parties insisted on conducting de facto vice-presidential elections by sharply differentiating between their presidential and vice-presidential entrants, and they rejected the antiparty idea of different parties controlling the two posts. The Twelfth Amendment in 1804 formalized the parties' position and repudiated the Framers' design. Since then, the thin and irregular provision of vice-presidential candidates of presumed presidential quality has been the leading complaint on the inadequacies of our presidential succession process.

The Framers' succession formula failed because its guarantee of a direct successor of presidential quality rested on a thorough rejection of the norm that the successor should be of the same party as the president. This "same-party criterion" is surely paramount in our day, but it should be noted that Congress has not always adhered to it when designating contingent successorship. For example, the

House Speaker and/or the Senate president pro tempore, put at the head of the line in the 1792 and 1947 acts, could be of a party other than the president's. Post-1967 reliance on the vice-president for both direct and contingent succession assures, of course, consistency with the same-party criterion.

The involvement of Congress in presidential successorship inevitably raises questions about possible intrusions on the separation of powers, but the record is rather stable and reassuring in this regard. Judging from past practices, the assignment of contingent succession to the two congressional leaders has not been considered an abridgment of the separation of powers. That verdict seems a bit sounder for the 1792 act, which called for a special presidential election, than for the 1947 act, under which the contingent successor completes the balance of the presidential term. Congress's post-1967 role with respect to contingent successorship is to confirm or reject the president's nominee to fill a vacated vice-presidency. How Congress handled that role in 1973 and 1974 will be discussed in a later chapter, but generally no upset of legislative-executive relations is threatened by any genuine and proper congressional exercise of its confirmation authority.[6] Finally, whatever disagreement

---

[6] It might be recalled that the Framers expected that often no presidential candidate would secure a majority of electoral votes, and that the House of Representatives would then be called on to choose the president from among the leading candidates. It happened not to work out that way, of

there may be over the wisdom of the policies adopted by Congress to deal with a vacant vice-presidency or a double vacancy, it is clear that Congress has not sought to misuse its constitutional authority on these matters to devise arrangements transgressing the separation of powers.

The last change meriting comment is that the president's role in determining successorship has become much more influential. As the Framers intended it, the runner-up presidential candidate would be the direct successor, and in situations of a double vacancy the top congressional leaders would be provisional contingent successors, with a special election to be held. This design obviously minimized the ability of an incumbent president to determine his own successorship. The changed character of the vice-presidency reflected in the Twelfth Amendment led at first to party leaders and then ultimately to the presidential candidate having the largest say in who the party's vice-presidential candidate would be. In that sense presidents over the past forty years have named their own immediate successor by controlling the nomination of their vice-presidential candidates. The electorate's role is not that of determining successorship directly but rather of choosing which set of paired presidential and vice-presidential contestants wins the election. Now that the

---

course, but the point remains that Congress's involvement in presidential succession is obviously lower than its anticipated involvement in presidential selection.

Twenty-fifth Amendment provides for a successor vice-president nominated by the president to be the contingent successor, presidential succession has come to rest essentially in the president's hands.

It would be difficult to overstate the importance of this trend for the analysis of the succession problem: the president's role in succession, negligible under the Framers, has become predominant in our time. Because of the dominance of the vice-presidency by the president, the hold of the vice-presidency on succession translates as a president's broad control over his own succession. The next stage of our inquiry, therefore, is to explore why presidential candidates have not been willing to select routinely as their potential successors vice-presidential candidates of presumed presidential quality. And if presidential candidates have been unwilling to do so, why have other major political actors and forces not persuaded or compelled them to honor that standard?

3

"Alternate Presidents": Needed but Unwanted

As the immediate successor to a vacated presidency, the vice-president should be of presidential quality. Eight of the nation's elected vice-presidents and the first of its appointed vice-presidents have inherited the highest office to complete the term; in all but two cases more than half the term remained. Of the thirteen presidents in the current century, eight were elected to office and five (38 percent) were vice-presidents who filled a vacated presidency caused by assassination (2), death by other causes (2), or resignation (1). And the Twenty-fifth Amendment, by assigning even contingent succession to the (appointed) vice-president, has made all the more compelling the need to select vice-presidents of presidential caliber.

Yet, as earlier discussed, the Twelfth Amendment in effect sacrificed the presidential quality of vice-presidents to protect the presidential quality of presidents. Whereas before the Twelfth Amendment two vice-presidents went on to win the

presidency, immediately afterward the secretary-
ship of state became the path to the White House.
Thereafter, presidential candidate recruitment
tapped a great variety of posts, but these did not
ordinarily include the vice-presidency until well
into the 1900s.[7]

During the 1800s, first-term vice-presidents
were routinely not renominated by their party, few
vice-presidents sought presidential nomination,
and all four vice-presidents who succeeded to a
vacated presidency were rejected by their party as
the next presidential nominee. Since 1804, only
one vice-president (Martin Van Buren) has advanced to the presidency by election directly after
completion of his vice-presidential term.

Vice-presidential nominating politics have reflected the low standing ot the post. Typically, the
number of competitors and the vigor of their
efforts have been slim and the extent of convention
division on the nomination has been small. More
than 75 percent of vice-presidential nominations
have been made on the first convention ballot. The
nominees themselves were broadly characterizable
as mediocrities, and those who won found little
opportunity in the office to develop contrary repu-
tations—from mediocrity to obscurity was the
customary progression. Are there many readers of

[7] Some modest qualification of these characterizations in
light of 20th-century trends will be offered later in this
section, but they require no serious amendment of the basic
description or of the core thesis as stated in the title of this
chapter.

this study who recognize any of the following as having served as vice-president: Daniel D. Tompkins, Richard M. Johnson, George Dallas, William R. King, Henry Wilson, William A. Wheeler, Levi P. Morton, Garrett A. Hobart, Thomas R. Marshall, or Charles Curtis?

So infirm a high public post has attracted a goodly share of ridicule. Observed Finley Peter Dunne's Mr. Dooley in cheerful denigration of the vice-presidency: "It wasn't a crime exactly. Ye can't be sint to jail f'r it, but it's a kind of disgrace. It's like writing anonymous letters." Crusty John Nance Garner, Franklin D. Roosevelt's vice-president in his first two terms, summed up that "the vice-presidency isn't worth a pitcher of warm spit." The essence of these and other barbed sallies about "the second highest office in the land" may be captured by applying to the vice-presidency Gertrude Stein's gibe against the city of Oakland, California: "There is no there there."

The formal position of the vice-president, who technically is neither a part of the executive branch nor subject to the direction of the president, underscores the anomaly of that office. Yet it would be too easy and misleading to dismiss the vice-presidency as a "nonjob." It is more instructive to treat the vice-presidency as a job defined by other political actors, especially though not exclusively by the president, but within tight constraints imposed by the American political system. That perspective leads one to ask why neither presidents nor the political system have made the vice-presidency into something that would better satisfy the widely acknowledged need for presidential-quality incumbency in that office. In providing answers we first sketch the subordination of the vice-president to the president, and then explore the seeming paradox of why vice-presidents of presidential caliber, though needed, are unwanted.

Subordination of the Vice-President: Nomination, Election, and Officeholding

Although vice-presidential candidates since 1804 have not been selected for their capacity to take on the presidency, control of their selection by the presidential candidate is of rather recent vintage. In the previous century, party leaders made the choice. William Jennings Bryan, a three-time losing Democratic presidential nominee, was close to the norm in his careful neglect each time to express a preference on who his running mate should be. Current practice, which is quite the opposite, was set by President Franklin D. Roosevelt at the time of his third-term nomination at the 1940 Democratic convention. Having failed to persuade Secretary of State Cordell Hull to accept the vice-presidential nomination, he forced the convention to accept Henry A. Wallace by threatening to resign the presidency otherwise. The tradition is now firm for the presidential nominee to select the vice-presidential candidate within a day after his own nomination and then to present that candidacy to the convention, which customarily provides overwhelming endorsement. On occasion a convention may dispute the choice, usually as a spillover of resentment about the presidential nomination, but the prevailing practice is automatic acquiescence, not revolt.

Vice-President Rockefeller assessed the political reality of vice-presidential selection accurately, in his November 3, 1975 letter to President Ford withdrawing his name from consideration for renomination in 1976:

Regarding next year and my own situation, I have made clear to you and to the public that I was not a candidate for the vice-presidency, that no one realistically can be such, and that the choice of a vice-presidential running mate is, and must be, up to the presidential candidate to recommend to a national party convention.

In picking their running mates, presidential nominees typically have sought to strengthen their chances of election by unifying their party for the campaign ahead. This has led them to adopt ticket-balancing strategies emphasizing regional, factional, ideological, or personal complementarity. Traditionally slighted has been consideration of who was most qualified to complete an unfinished presidential term and, all too often, of whether the person chosen to balance the ticket was even minimally qualified for successorship. To the extent that the ticket was designed to appeal to divergent factions and interests for election purposes, it helped assure that the president, once in office, would find little

use to make of a vice-president who had profoundly dissimilar views from his own. And should
such a vice-president succeed to a vacated presidency, major policy discontinuity could result, notwithstanding their common party label. But the
essential characteristic of vice-presidential selection
was precisely that such postelection concerns were
deemed beside the point. As Representative James
G. O'Hara (Democrat, Michigan) has nicely put it:
"Whether they should or not, [presidential candi-
dates] will not, in the final analysis, choose their
vice-presidential candidate to succeed them. They
will choose them to help them succeed."[8]

At the election stage, the party's national ticket
must be responded to as a ticket, precluding voters
from supporting a presidential and vice-presidential candidate of different parties. The ticket, however, is no team of coequals. The vice-presidential
candidate is more an appendage than a partner of
the presidential contestant, in terms of voter per-
ception and impact on the election.[9] Because the
vice-presidential race is not separate, and because it

[8] Testimony before the Special Commission on Vice-
Presidential Selection of the Democratic National Commit-
tee, 7 November 1973 (mimeo), p. 10; quoted by Schlesinger,
Jr., "On the Presidential Succession," p. 484.

[9] The evidence suggests the vice-presidential candidate
adds little electoral strength to the ticket in his home state and
that "balance" is of little utility to the ticket with respect to
direct voter impact. See, for example, Carl B. Tubbesing,
"Vice-Presidential Candidates and the Home State Advantage:
Or 'Tom Who?' Was Tom Eagleton in Missouri," *Western
Political Quarterly* 26 (Dec. 1973): 702-716.

is "decided" only indirectly and distantly as a by-product of the decision made on the presidential contest, it can be seriously questioned whether the vice-president is an elected official in the customary meaning of that term.

The mode of appraisal of the vice-presidency as an office was set by John Adams, our first vice-president, who characterized it as "the most insignificant office that ever the invention of man contrived or his imagination conceived." It was not until Warren Harding's brief administration that the vice-president became a regular attender at Cabinet meetings, a practice reinstituted by Franklin Roosevelt (although Cabinet meetings themselves seem to have gone out of style under contemporary presidents). Beyond that symbolic Cabinet attendance, the activity, visibility, and utility of a vice-president have turned on the wishes of his president. Most presidents have wished to do little for the vice-president and to have the vice-president do little for them. In 1960, for example, when President Eisenhower was asked by a reporter to give an example of a major policy contributed by Richard Nixon (his vice-president and the then Republican presidential candidate) to Ike's administration, the President replied, "If you give me a week, I might think of one." Typically, neither their personal nor collegial relations are close: the political wag, Art Buchwald, wrote a column in late 1974 about a vice-president who had to pretend he was the father of the March of Dimes poster child just to get into the president's office.

The relationship between president and vice-president is asymmetrical, then, with the former calling the tune at every turn. An apt example is provided by Nelson Rockefeller, an aggressive and experienced public official whose political standing was higher than that of Gerald Ford before the latter was appointed vice-president and then succeeded to the presidency. Once Rockefeller became President Ford's appointed vice-president, he and his staff spoke candidly of the sharp constraints on his new role, constraints that spoke to the office itself and not to the nonelective path by which he had come to it.

Question: Americans seem to be drifting, or maybe searching for leadership. How are you going to turn this around? Can you exert leadership from this office?
Rockefeller: I am not going to. I am not in a leadership position. I am supporting the president. He can exert the leadership and I can support him.

Summed up one of Rockefeller's aides about the new vice-president, "He understands very thoroughly that he is whatever the president says he is."[10] That posture covered even the one power assigned to the vice-president by the Constitution, that of presiding over the Senate. In early 1975, another Senate effort to modify the filibuster procedures (Rule 22) was mounted, and it required the Chair (Rockefeller) to make strategic parliamentary rulings. "On January 10th," Rockefeller noted to novelist-reporter John

[10] *Time*, 20 January 1975, p. 23, for both the question and response and the aide's quote.

Hersey, who was monitoring the White House to develop an account of one week of the president's activities, "I asked the president how he wanted Rule 22 handled."

As an official with a fixed term of office who in form is independently elected, the vice-president theoretically could break out from obscurity by acting autonomously. Such a departure would make good media copy and give prominence, if not notoriety, to the vice-president. But such a move would require considerable political sustenance, which almost surely would have to take the form of the vice-president's alliance with a party or congressional faction at odds with the president, that is, covert or overt opposition to the president (disloyalty) would be involved or implied. This would be a very high-risk route for the vice-president to choose, which doubtless accounts for the complete absence of takers among the vice-presidents of recent decades.

In practice, the vice-president has come to accept his dependence on his president's willingness to assign him significant functions. But that willingness invariably has strings attached, namely, that the vice-president will be permitted to exercise those functions only as a subordinate agent of the president. And the functions themselves typically will relate to the political rather than the policy-making needs of the president, such as symbolic-ceremonial visitations and speechmaking, party maintenance, developing public and congressional support for administration proposals, and helping the first-term president secure re-election. Hence the costs to the vice-president of being rescued from oblivion may come high. Acting as the president's man, the vice-president may find himself having to endorse personally uncongenial policies, to develop an image helpful to the president but not necessarily to himself, and generally to handicap as much as to help his future prospects and ambitions. Such a circumscribed role inhibits the vice-president from demonstrating the full range of his talents and from expressing his genuine policy preferences, so that no reliable estimates of his overall qualities and outlook can confidently be made on the basis of his record as vice-president. The more effective his performance as a presidential agent, the less the public can determine what his own views are on matters on which he is advocating his principal's cause. At the extreme, if what the vice-president is called on to do on behalf of the president is persistently and profoundly at variance with his own beliefs, the experience could be so demeaning and debilitating as to produce at the close of the four-year term someone less qualified for the presidency than he was before becoming vice-president.

This characterization of the vice-president in office should not be drawn too starkly or negatively. Tolerant presidents, sure-footed vice-presidents, and the right mix of circumstances have combined to give some vice-presidents visibility and a leadership reputation of sorts. In the 1900s as compared with the previous century, nearly all incumbent vice-presidents were renominated for a second term and more sought presidential nomination. All four post-1900 elected vice-presidents who succeeded to the presidency easily won presidential nomination in their own right and then went on to election victory—a record that comments as much, however, on the expanding role of the presidency as it does on the vice-presidency. Recent evidence is suggestive, though mixed, on whether the vice-presidency is coming to be seen routinely as a base from which to launch a serious presidential candidacy.

Even if the modern vice-presidency is judged to be increasing in importance, albeit slowly, unevenly, and more in the sense of greater prominence and publicity than power, that office is or will become, at most, but one of the diverse recruitment sources for presidential aspirants. Further, its incumbents will continue to find—in the manner of Vice-President Hubert Humphrey's "entrapment" in President Lyndon Johnson's 1965-1968 position on America's war in Vietnam—that the prominence gained by being associated in the public mind with the president's administration is a two-edged sword. Finally, whether or not vice-presidents are using that post more frequently to press for a presidential nomination, it still remains true that vice-presidential nominees seldom are selected because their perceived talents and standing *at the time they are chosen* qualify them to complete a presidential term, and that vice-presidents can function significantly, if at all, only in the narrowly circumscribed role of administration agent. The explanation for these conditions relates to the American political system and hence tells us something basic about the source and shape of the succession problem.

No Place for an "Alternate President"

From the point of view of the presidential candidate/president there is neither need nor incentive to choose a vice-presidential candidate/vice-president who has and will maintain an independent power base, who is acknowledged to possess presidential standing *before* assuming the vice-presidential office, or who, because his general reputation is that of an "alternate president," must be taken as a rival of the president himself. Clearly, the president's interests run in the opposite direction altogether, toward limited and controlled use of *his* running mate and *his* vice-president as but one of *his* subordinates and spokesmen. Political necessity (not an explicit search for qualified successorship) may on occasion lead a presidential candidate to tap a major competitor as his running mate, but when in office the president will then cut his rival down to size, subordination, and/or relative obscurity, for example, Kennedy and Johnson, Johnson and Humphrey.[11] For his part, the vice-presidential

[11] Johnson's acceptance of Kennedy's invitation to be his vice-presidential candidate (an invitation the Kennedy camp expected him to turn down) surely marked the decline if not the end of LBJ's standing as a presidential competitor. As vice-president, Johnson greatly resented his thorough exclusion from the policy centers of the administration, a situation of

candidate/vice-president understands all too well—
as the previous quotations of and about Nelson
Rockefeller indicate—that he lacks the capacity to
define an effective role independent of service to the
president or on terms other than those satisfactory
to the president.

Like the president, neither major party can accept
contentedly the regular occurrence of situations
where vice-presidential candidates/vice-presidents
are chosen in clear recognition of their presidential
caliber. That recognition, together with the advan-
tages accruing from being the vice-president, would
stamp the incumbent as the front-running candidate for his party's next available presidential
nomination, especially during the president's final
term. Other presidential hopefuls of the White
House party would resent and resist such a fore-
closure of the competition. Similarly, the out-party
would oppose so significant an edge in the next
presidential race being given to the in-party's vice-
president.[12]

---

growing isolation from which he was rescued by his succession
to the presidency when Kennedy was assassinated.

[12] Recall, for example, the opposition expressed within
both parties to the possibility that President Nixon might fill
the vice-presidency vacated in 1973 by Agnew with one of the
leading Republican presidential aspirants. There was even
some short-lived talk among Democrats about barring from
presidential candidacy in 1976 anyone Nixon nominated to be
vice-president. As another example, plausible speculation had
it that President Ford appointed Nelson Rockefeller as his
vice-president in part to neutralize or eliminate him as a major
presidential rival within the Republican party.

In American politics, presidential availability and recruitment are not confined narrowly to a few jump-off positions or to a career ladder of fixed, sequential political posts. The vice-presidency, as mentioned earlier, may be in process of becoming more of a presidential jump-off point but, even so, it will still be only one of many. If, however, the vice-president were widely perceived as having earned his nomination, election, and office *because* of his preexisting high political standing and presidential qualifications, he would come to be seen as the "heir apparent" in his party. Confining the vice-presidency to persons of recognized presidential caliber (and presidential ambitions) thus would have the effect, however unintended, of promoting the vice-presidency as an office with dominant claims on the in-party's next open presidential nomination. Broad, intense political opposition to such a development surely would emerge and, whatever its mix of motives, such opposition would have a strong case on the merits of the matter.

In pursuing remedies for America's succession problem, reformers persistently have sought ways to structure the choice of vice-presidential candidates to assure, as a regular result, the tapping of persons of presumed presidential quality. Reformers have been able to count on widespread, albeit not intense, support for the idea of high-quality successorship. And there has been and is nothing in the party convention's rules that would preclude that outcome; party leaders, the presidential nominee, and/or the convention delegates are not confined in their canvass or choice. Yet throughout our history achievement of that objective has been the exception and not the rule.

Reformers are wont to rest the explanation on the shortsightedness, selfishness, or folly of party and political leaders and to exhort such leaders to change and to do "the right and needed thing." Although there may well be a grain of truth in this reformers' perspective, so consistent a pattern of vice-presidential selection suggests a different explanation. Such a pattern surely indexes a basic conflict or contradiction within the political system itself. Whereas the satisfaction of successorship needs requires vice-presidents of the quality of "alternate presidents," our political system provides no viable role for an "alternate president" in addition to the president. The typical outcome of this enduring conflict demonstrates that the dysfunctional liabilities of a "president-like" vice-president have been considered more compelling than the benefits of securing that successorship objective.

The disincentives to sustaining a practice of selecting presidential-quality vice-presidents are rooted in the structure and dynamics of our political system—and hence they are not amenable to change by exhortation or by institutional tinkering. It is not, for example, the jealousies of individual presidents that account for the absence of shared power with vice-presidents, but rather the indivisibility of presidential leadership and the lack of place for tandem governance by two. As the importance and power of

the presidency increased, so did the need for
effective successorship, but the marginal, subordinate, and essentially anomalous role of the vice-
president underwent no appreciable change. Consider, as another example, the relative unattractive-
ness of a vice-presidential nomination to major
presidential-caliber leaders who already have an
independent power base. To act as a subordinate
service agent of the president would surely not be
much of an attraction. They would not seek the vice-
presidency on their own initiative, and they likely
would be ambivalent about accepting a presidential
candidate's invitation to be his running mate. If they
were persuaded to become the vice-presidential
nominee and then won, their circumscribed and
controlled stint as vice-president might as likely
tarnish as burnish the lustre they had prior to taking
that office. Or if they tried to become a more
autonomous vice-president by capitalizing on their
own initial prominence, the system-based opposition of other major political actors to that development would make the attempt unstable at best, and
very possibly would make it a self-destructive route
for the vice-president to follow.

Although this analysis has focused on the vice-
presidency, the force of its themes is in no way
limited just to that post. Its applicability extends to
any other office one might suggest, whether already
existing or yet to be created, whose *primary* function
is to provide high-quality successorship to a vacated
presidency. The systemic reasons that explain why
the vice-presidency has not operated as a reliable

source of supply of presidential successors of presumed presidential quality also explain why a reliance on any alternate office would do no better. In sum, it is the inhospitality of our political system, not the pettiness of our political leaders, that best accounts for the inability to produce "alternate presidents" on a regular basis, which would be one way the felt need for presidential-quality successorship could be satisfied.

An Indirect "Alternate President"?

If the objective of providing an "alternate president" is not met by establishing a post directly for that purpose, can it be accomplished indirectly? This would involve assigning immediate presidential successorship to a public office with its own impressive standing and authority independent of its successorship role, and whose occupant, therefore, would likely to be of acknowledged presidential quality. The post should be one that attracts or recruits persons of demonstrated political quality, that further develops its incumbent's political skills and repute, and that is perceived by the public as warranting first claim on successorship.

However compelling the logic of this approach, there appears no way to implement it effectively. Only a handful of posts would seem to merit consideration at all: on the elective side, the top two congressional leaders and, on the appointive side, the leading Cabinet heads or the chief justice of the Supreme Court. (To satisfy the same-party criterion, the first and third of these possibilities would require amendment to condition the incumbent's succession on his being of the same party as that of the president.) Whichever post was chosen, those determining who was to fill it would be required to engage in a balance of considerations so delicate and ambiguous as to assure only partial success at best. The person would have to be chosen with primary but not exclusive concern for his ability to handle the important office itself and with some significant but not overriding concern for his capacity to conduct the presidency effectively. Aggravating the difficulties would be the underlying troubling question of whether the qualities making for a skilled handling of the functions of the designated office were readily transferable to what the presidency required.

A review of who in recent decades has occupied the posts mentioned, or of who occupies them today, generates little confidence that the incumbents of any of them would usually, much less invariably, be considered to be of presidential quality. Further, although one or another of these posts, with the exception of the chief justiceship, has served for some period in our history as first contingent successor to a vacated presidency, little attention has been paid to that aspect of the office when determining who would fill it. Our political system, in short, can no more be counted on to produce indirect than direct alternate presidents.

The nub of the position here advanced is that the long-time quest for presidential-quality succession has proved illusory because it took the form of seeking to embed an alternate president in a political system which was understandably unreceptive, if not outrightly hostile, to such a post. As a consequence, the vice-presidency has operated in conformity to the system's dynamics and not as a supplier of presidential-quality successors. If that line of analysis is valid, two broad directions of possible solution remain to be explored. One direction in effect reinsists on meeting the objective of alternate presidents, by upgrading the quality of vice-presidents through strengthening the position of the vice-presidential candidate and/or the authority of the vice-presidency. This direction involves, as it must, efforts to breach the systemic constraints that thus far have undercut achieving the objective. Numerous and varied proposals fall into this category, which will be described and reviewed in the next chapter. The other direction, to be taken up now, considers it futile or undesirable to institutionalize alternate presidents, and in effect returns to the Framers' logic to come up with a modern equivalent of their solution to the problem.

A Special Presidential Election

The central insight of the Framers' design was that presidential elections would produce not only presidents of presumed presidential quality but presidential-quality vice-presidents as well, to whom succession would be assigned. That would be accomplished by holding a presidential competition only, and by awarding the vice-presidency (the presidential successorship post) to the major losing candidate. The premise underlying the Framer's design ran afoul in its day of a growing commitment to the same-party norm. The democratic values expressed by that norm are so solidly rooted in our contemporary political culture as to preclude any literal reintroduction of the Framers' solution. The runner-up presidential candidate in the general election thus cannot be placed at the head of the succession line. To provide the functional equivalent of the Framers' design consistent with our values, presidential successorship would have to occur by special election of a new president in place of assigning succession to the vice-president (or any other office).

It may be useful to recapitulate in summary form the progression of the analysis:

1. Regular presidential elections can consistently produce vice-presidents of presidential quality (the runner-up presidential candidate) only by violating the same-party criterion.

2. Regular vice-presidential elections typically can produce vice-presidents of either

    a. presumed presidential quality (this has not happened because of conflict with the dynamics of the political system) or

    b. presumed nonpresidential quality (this has been the pattern).

Because #1 is not acceptable, and #2b rather than #2a has prevailed, the solution lies in severing the connection between succession and the vice-presidency and in reassigning succession to the winner of a special presidential election.[13]

Congress already has authority under article 2, section 1 to provide by statute for such special elections, although repeal of parts of the Twenty-fifth Amendment would be required also. Consideration of the problems involved in the setting up of special presidential elections is beyond the scope of this short study, but a few examples might be helpful to the reader. What should be the date of the election relative to the date of presidential vacancy? A long time period would be fairer to potential candidates and third parties, but a shorter period would reduce the time of public uncertainty and of governance by a transitory caretaker. Again, how to treat provisional successorship raises a cluster of important concerns. Who should it be, and should this person have full or partial authority as an interim acting president? Should he be allowed to run in the special election and, if so, how might that affect the conduct of his provisional presidency and the unity of his party? As a final example, should a special election be held no matter how brief the balance of the

---

[13] The same view is swiftly reached, without need for complicated analysis, from another viewpoint as yet unmentioned. Stressing the importance of the presidency and what in their view popular sovereignty requires, some urge that the only legitimate president is one who is elected to be president. No successorship office, regardless of the presumed presidential quality of its incumbent, would be acceptable. This view, not widely held, obviously converts presidential succession into a nonproblem.

uncompleted term?[14] If not, then how should the
arrangements for provisional succession in that
situation differ from those applied to successorship
that is followed by a special election? Clearly, these
and other difficult problems would have to be
worked out in connection with use of special
presidential elections, but none appears so severe as
to warrant rejection, on those grounds, of this
proposed solution.

There is a more fundamental question, however,
which ultimately the reader must decide for himself
or herself. Is it wise to mandate a special election,
given the diverse circumstances that might attach to
a presidential vacancy? For example, would it have
been more advantageous or more harmful, on
balance, to have followed President Nixon's resignation in midsummer 1974 by a special election
rather than by the automatic succession of the vice-
president? What of the situation of a vacated
presidency occasioned by the impeachment and
conviction of the incumbent? Or brought about by
the assassination of the president? It should be
emphasized that these are not rhetorical questions
permitting but a single answer, and judgments on
them surely would differ. At least two inferences
should be evident. The first is that a preference for

[14] The successor, whether it be the vice-president as under
current practice or the newly elected president as suggested
by this proposal, should serve to complete the vacated term
rather than take on a new four-year term. The schedule of
national elections as set in the Constitution is an integral part
of our checks-and-balances scheme.

special elections should rest not solely on the capacity of that means to satisfy the objective of securing presidential-quality succession but on a favorable net assessment of its larger range of positive and negative effects. The second inference is that those who are persuaded that the potential risks and disabilities of a special election outweigh its benefits, and therefore reject that solution, must move to redefine the primary goal of succession in terms other than its provision of presidential-quality successors. That redefinition and its application will occupy our attention in the fifth chapter of this study.

WHAT ABOUT THE VICE-PRESIDENCY?

Any effort to gain adoption of the special election device would have to deal with the question of what to do about the vice-presidency. As it was the failings of that office which necessitated the turn to special presidential elections, the general disposition to abandon the vice-presidency might well be high. Surely if that office were denied the provisional successorship role most would see it as having become a superfluous post ripe for elimination. It is conceivable that if the vice-president were made provisional successor the office could be continued as before, but sentiment for its demise might nonetheless remain strong. It is one thing, after all, to accept the takeover of the presidency by the vice-president in the context of automatic succession and no election. It is quite another, however, to accept that takeover in the context of a forthcoming election, for the vice-president as interim president would likely seek to foreclose the competition by capturing his party's presidential nomination for himself and by using the powers of the presidency on behalf of his nomination and election bid. Still, the problem posed inheres in provisional successorship as such and is not peculiar to the vice-president as provisional successor. If the provisional successor is not to be the vice-president, who else should it be? In the absence of a ready alternative, the vice-presidency might be unenthusiastically retained, notwithstanding the adoption of the special election mechanism to provide full successorship.

4

Key Constraints Violated: Undesirable Reforms of the Vice-Presidency

Although proposals to change one or another aspect of the vice-presidency are numerous and diverse, most share a common intent and direction. They continue the vice-presidency and keep it as an elective office, but they try to take it out from under the shadow of the presidential candidate/president and to make it a more prominent and prestigious post in its own right. To that end a multitude of suggestions have been offered which would alter the mode of vice-presidential nomination or election, or would expand the power of the vice-president. Their common logic may be put as follows: if the office is made more substantial and given a more independent and positive identity, its character may be transformed sufficiently to attract to it high-quality leaders who would satisfy the need for presidential-caliber successorship. Considered in isolation, this proposition appears unexceptionable. When it is placed in systemic context, however, judgment is likely to be rather different. The

purpose of the analysis that follows is to evaluate a
representative selection of these proposed reforms,
with due attention paid to that systemic context.

Key Constraints

How one appraises proposed changes in the vice-
presidency turns, of course, on the criteria one uses,
which then become constraints defining the limits
of acceptable reform. The key constraints developed
here are drawn from the systemic analysis presented
in the previous chapter. Reforms which are found to
violate the key constraints are likely, because of that
contradiction, to operate quite differently from their
intent and are certain to dissatisfy other important
needs and values. Such reforms, therefore, are here
judged to be undesirable changes which should not
be adopted.

SAME-PARTY CONTROL

The first key constraint is that a presidential
successor should be of the same party as the last
president. This constraint squares with our post-
Twelfth Amendment practice with respect to the
vice-presidency. The vice-presidential and presidential candidacies have been paired as a joint ticket,
thus precluding cross-party results as long as each
major party chooses its nominees from within its
own ranks. Two exceptions, but of the kind that
prove the rule, have occurred. The Whigs in 1840
and the Republicans in 1864 named a Democrat as

their vice-presidential nominee in an effort to increase their voting strength; in the latter instance the Republicans even temporarily abandoned their name—during the Civil War—and became the Union party. In both cases the party won but, as luck would have it, the president died and the vice-president, a member of the opposition party, succeeded to the office. Since then, parties have avoided such strategic risks and have kept their vice-presidential nominations within the fold.

Virtually all proposed reforms respect this constraint and eschew arrangements which would or could result in the president and vice-president being of different parties. Why this constraint should be honored can best be explained by reviewing two reforms that go in the opposite direction. One would mandate a different-party outcome, and the other would permit it by voter decision.

An occasional contemporary voice is heard in support of reestablishing the Framers' plan whereby the vice-presidency would be awarded to the runner-up in the presidential race. It is of little concern, in this view, how a vice-presidency housing the opposition party leader would function. Same-party vice-presidents, after all, have not operated as indispensable public officials, and hence no great loss of function would be involved. The important thing, concludes this view, is to have a presidential-quality successor, and this change would accomplish that.

One response is to question what such a vice-president could do in office. If he were isolated and without function, his stint as vice-president would become, in effect, an "exile in silence" that would erode his leadership role, the same role that was the basis for assigning the vice-presidency to him in the first place. On the other hand, should he attempt to operate actively within the executive branch as the leader of the opposition, this would involve so novel and problematic a form of governance as to raise concerns far graver than the quality of presidential successorship.

Another response is to emphasize that the same-party criterion speaks to the values of party responsibility and governance and of popular sovereignty, and to their mutual relationship. As slack as our party system may be when compared to European types, it still serves as the major mechanism linking the public and government, structuring governance, and subjecting the government of the day to review and opposition. It would violate the integrity of the party system to shape election to the most important governmental office in a way that would mandate giving the office, if it were vacated, over to the opposition party. The same point can be made from the closely related viewpoint of adherence to the basic democratic norm of popular sovereignty. The electorate's verdict would be overturned, and hence betrayed, if successorship were assigned to a presidential candidate defeated in the last election. Accordingly, one change that is clearly unacceptable would be to hold a presidential election only, with electors limited to casting one vote and with the seccond-running candidate declared the vice-president.

What of a proposal, however, that is consistent with popular sovereignty, such as one which provides for separate vice-presidential and presidential elections and which thereby makes it possible for voters to elect a president and vice-president of different parties? A purist's fidelity to popular sovereignty might lead one to insist on allowing that option, rather than foreclosing it as present arrangements do. In a democracy, after all, the people have a right "to go to hell in a handbasket," if that is what they wish to do. But our political system—like others—shapes and constrains the exercise of popular sovereignty on behalf of other values and goals deemed important. For example, we very deliberately elect our national Representatives by single-member districts and plurality vote, not by proportional representation. This reflects our greater commitment to the values of two-partyism and stability of governance than to an arithmetically faithful representation of the range and distribution of viewpoints in the citizenry. It would seem no less justifiable to constrict citizen choice to assure a president and vice-president of the same party, on grounds of the party's role in national governance and the successorship role of the vice-president.

In spite of the compelling rationale for the same-party constraint, Congress has departed from it in setting contingent successorship, and that deficiency should be corrected. The successor role of the House Speaker and the Senate president pro tempore should be conditioned on conformity to the

same-party criterion; they should be passed over for
succession when not of the president's party. It is
appropriate for cabinet heads to be successors as
long as the president has confined the appointments to members of his own party. Similarly, the
Twenty-fifth Amendment provision for filling a
vacated vice-presidency is also satisfactory, on the
reasonable assumptions that the president will
nominate someone of his own party and that
Congress, even when controlled by the opposition
party, will honor the president's right to do so.

POLICY DISCONTINUITY NOT ENCOURAGED

Successorship that meets the same-party standard
may nonetheless involve policy discontinuity because of the nature of American parties. Although
our two major parties differ on their modal policy
positions, either party taken alone encompasses a
wide range of policy views. It would presumably
make a real difference in what national policy
objectives were pursued whether, for example,
Nelson Rockefeller or Ronald Reagan, or George
Wallace or Edmund Muskie succeeded to a vacated
presidency.[15] This suggests the desirability of adding to the same-party constraint the requirement
that the successor have, broadly, the same policy
outlook as the last president. Because voters have

[15] It bears reminding, however, that the behavior of vice-
presidents after succession to the presidency is often difficult
to predict. Both the office and the policy goals of the departed
president may have profound effects on the successor.

never really selected the vice-president in any direct, clear way, the electoral verdict in the last presidential election provides the citizenry's latest policy mandate, which a presidential successor should honor. Popular sovereignty, in other words, also is the justification for this new constraint as well. Further, a vice-president of profoundly dissimilar policy views to those of the president would be in an unenviable position when in office, having to choose between being ignored by the president or giving up his own policy preferences to support those of the president.

There are insuperable difficulties, however, in implementing a constraint formulated affirmatively to require policy continuity. To provide but one example, the presidential candidate's position on many policy matters often may be ambiguous or thinly formed, and his actions as president may deviate considerably from his policy stands during the campaign. It makes sense, therefore, to reformulate the constraint to read negatively: presidential succession arrangements should not make probable policy discontinuity between a successor president and his predecessor within the same presidential term.

Application of this constraint would rule out any mode of nominating or electing the vice-president which would likely result in the second spot on the ticket going to a policy opponent of the presidential nominee. A number of reform proposals, discussed later in this chapter, are vulnerable to the charge of violating this constraint. So, too, is the assignment of contingent successorship to the top legislative leaders regardless of their party. The use of Cabinet heads as contingent successors, in contrast, falls within the constraint. Present arrangements on immediate successorship are also satisfactory in that the presidential nominee has enough influence and discretion in the selection of the vice-presidential candidate to work within this contraint if he wishes to and if circumstances permit. Indeed, there may be developing a greater tendency for presidential candidates to choose running mates in part because they have a similar policy outlook, for example, Truman/Barkley (1948), Johnson/Humphrey (1964), Goldwater/Miller (1964), Nixon/Agnew (1968, 1972), McGovern/Shriver (1972). It bears reemphasis, however, that the constraint under discussion requires only that the nominating process not encourage the selection of a running mate who is a policy foe of the presidential candidate, and not that it guarantee selection of a policy ally.

PRESIDENTIAL DISCRETION AND CONTROL

A third constraint affirms as an appropriate norm what in fact has developed with respect to the preeminence of the presidency and its predominance over the vice-presidency. It reflects the reality that the president cannot be expected to nuture within his own party rival leadership that would challenge his standing as *the* political, party, and governmental leader. Nor does the political system, as distinct from the incumbent president, encourage or sustain such dual leadership. This constraint also expresses the priority choice embodied in the Twelfth Amendment and confirmed throughout our subsequent political history: an upgrading of the vice-presidency is not acceptable if it involves a downgrading of the presidency. Stated affirmatively, this constraint requires that the presidential nominee have considerable discretion and the controlling say in the designation of a running mate and that the president have considerable discretion and the controlling say in the determination of the activities of the vice-president.

This constraint rests on a principled justification as well, not merely on the pragmatics of how our political system operates. Succession should be seen more as filling a vacated office than simply a vacant one, more as completing an interrupted term of office than as beginning a new, abbreviated one. It is the departed president, after all, and not his successor, who represents the most recent popular verdict on the presidency. His successor, therefore, should be one acceptable to him and sensitive to the policy preferences of his administration. In this sense, the closest functional approximation to a special presidential election is to structure succession so as to make more probable the successor's continuation of the last president's programs. Assuring the president a dominant role in the designation of his successor obviously promotes that objective, though it cannot guarantee achieving it.

Undesirable Reforms of the Vice-Presidency

Adherence to this constraint sharply limits the range of acceptable reform of the vice-presidency. Those proposed changes which seek to "purify" the means by which presidential control would be exercised pass the test, but those which aim to dilute or displace that dominance do not. As most reforms of the vice-presidency move in the direction of a greater insulation of that office from direct control of the president/presidential nominee, they violate the constraints in varying degree and hence are deemed undesirable. Their unacceptability is most pronounced when applied to the quite common situation of an administration running for a second term, when ordinarily the incumbent president has sewed up his renomination, and that of his vice-president, well in advance of the convention and unquestionably dominates both his party and the executive branch. When fitted to such circumstances, many of the reform proposals are simply incongruous and, whatever their merits otherwise, are unfeasible. This notice of a general deficiency is intended to serve in lieu of burdening the reader with repetitive commentary to that effect for each reform reviewed in the analysis that follows. For the same reason the analysis will emphasize the situation of presidential nominees in quest of their first term, with readers left on their own to complement the account by adding the situation of incumbent presidents pursuing their second term.

INCREASING THE AUTHORITY OF THE
VICE-PRESIDENT

If, through passage of a constitutional amendment, the powers assigned to the vice-presidency were expanded, would not the office become more attractive to high-quality political leaders? And would not the experience and knowledge gained by vice-presidents who had important tasks to perform prepare them better for the presidency, should circumstances require their succession to that office? Such appealing logic underlies proposals which seek to enlarge the authority base of the vice-president. Two examples illustrate the genre. One proposal would empower the vice-president to vote on all issues before the Senate, in place of his present confinement to instances of tie votes. Another proposal would formally make the vice-president a member of the executive branch, and then either would assign him to specific important duties or "require" the presidential nominee to pledge that he would, as president, make the vice-president head of a Cabinet department.

Neither proposal, once placed into context, makes much sense. The first is mistaken in that the preparatory experience needed by a presidential successor is in the executive branch, not the Senate. Less obviously, it errs in assuming that a vice-president would welcome or could make effective autonomous use of the opportunity (or the burden?) of being on public record on any matter voted on by the Senate. The most likely outcome would be to compel the vice-president to make more visible and automatic his advocacy role as agent of the administration, which is scarcely calculated to promote the independent authority of the office or reputation of its incumbent. If the vice-president chose to deviate markedly from that role, it would undercut his utility to the president and violate the constraints that a presidential successor should seek to follow the policy directions of his predecessor. Most basically, the proposal fails to understand that in the conduct of his newly expanded Senate role the vice-president would have neither electoral nor moral mandate to "be his own man" rather than the president's man.

The second proposal is more sensible than the first in its embedding of the vice-president in the executive branch, but it is no less deficient. The Constitution vests an undivided "executive power" in the president, which translates politically into the requirement that the top leadership echelons of the executive branch must be accountable to the president. But a vice-president, who in form is also elected for the same fixed four-year term as the president, could not be held to that standard of accountability if he were irremovably in charge of a designated set of important functions and/or an executive department. It would be helpful, of course, for presidents to prepare vice-presidents for possible succession by involving them in substantial policy or administrative matters. But attempts to mandate significant independent authority for the vice-president must involve, however unintendedly, coercion of the president to compel his use of the vice-president in a certain way or an institutionalization of a rival power base within the executive which may challenge presidential leadership and responsibility, or both. Any such "reform" would be both unwelcome and unstable and, if it were ever to gain adoption, it would assuredly not work out as intended.

It should be noted that the practical case for a greater separation of the vice-presidential from the presidential election rests heavily on converting the vice-presidency into a substantial post with considerable authority of its own. Otherwise, high-quality leaders would not seek it, and voters would have little basis on which to choose. Because systemic contraints militate against transforming the authority of the vice-president, the election of the vice-president should be kept closely connected to that of the president.

PRECONVENTION NOMINATING CHANGES

A number of proposals that differ in their particulars share the objective of making the nomination of a vice-presidential candidate a public and prominent matter in its own right. By getting the public to focus early on the vice-presidency *per se,* these preconvention nomination reforms hope to make the office more attractive to prospective candidates, to stimulate the emergence of a distinct group of high-quality contestants for the post, and to provide the basis for a more thoughtful and deliberate choice of the nominee.

Set 1 proposals: One set of proposals would separate the nomination of vice-presidents from that of presidents. One example is the suggestion that separate vice-presidential primaries be established, and that the convention choose its vice-presidential nominee from among those who entered such primaries.[16] Another proposal calls for simultaneous national presidential and vice-presidential primaries, with the convention limited, presumably, to *pro forma* ratification of the winners.

Set 2 proposals: Another set of proposals pursues the same objective by requiring the creation of linked candidacies—presidential and vice-presidential—before the convention meets. One notion would institutionalize slate contests in party primaries, with the entrants competing as presidential and vice-presidential tickets. Another would require a presidential hopeful to designate his intended running mate several months in advance of the convention. In either case, the convention would make its choice from among the already-formed presidential/vice-presidential tickets. A third version would have each presidential contender make public, well before the outset of the convention, a list of three or four persons he would find acceptable as his running mate. The convention would then choose the vice-presidential nominee from the successful presidential candidate's list.

[16] The use of primaries as the nominating device has provoked much debate and disagreement, but that issue is not central to my line of analysis and hence I have not included it.

Both sets of proposed reforms are doubly defective—in their own terms and because they contradict key constraints. By forcing prospective aspirants to choose early between their presidential and vice-presidential hopes (and chances), the likeliest outcome would be to impoverish the quality of candidates for the vice-presidency. This is, after all, *the* perennial problem of the anomalous post of the vice-presidency, the one that has confounded every generation of reformers, the Framers included. Rather than compete for or accept the vice-presidential nomination *before* the presidential nomination is made, first-rate leaders are likely to remove themselves from the candidacy pool for vice-president.

This defect can be plugged by yet another proposal, one which takes a leaf from the Framers' book. Why not jettison a direct contest for the vice-presidential nomination and rely, instead, on assigning the second spot on the ticket to the runner-up in a national presidential primary?[17] But this remedy, like any other in set 1 that would thoroughly insulate the vice-presidential choice from control by the presidential candidate, is basically flawed. Under present arrangements, the reference point for constructing a national ticket is the freshly chosen presidential candidate. These proposals, however, would eliminate any reference point, either by determining the vice-presidential

---

[17] Unlike the Framers' plan, however, it cannot be safely assumed that the runner-up would always be willing to accept the vice-presidential nomination.

nominee in advance and independent of the designation of the presidential nominee or by insisting, regardless of who the presidential nominee was, that the runner-up presidential contender be his running mate. The result would often be less a genuine ticket than the sum of two unrelated candidacies. The possibilities for promoting incompatible marriages of ideological or policy opponents obviously would be high, in clear contravention of the second of the three constraints earlier discussed.

In practice, the premise of the first set of proposals—the insulation of the vice-presidential from the presidential nominating process—is likely to be undercut if the timing and form of the vice-presidential primary permit the intervention of presidential aspirants. The latter would likely convert the vice-presidential race into a test of their own relative strengths. Such a development could well result in the worst of both worlds: the vice-presidential contest could become the object of manipulation by presidential rivals, while convention and public judgments of the presidential contenders would turn in part on the complicated and somewhat unpredictable happenings in the secondary arena of the struggle for the vice-presidential nomination. To be sure, the vice-presidency would gain a new visibility and public focus, but it would be of a rather different kind than these proposals had in mind.

Set 2, unlike set 1, provides for ticket construction. Presidential and vice-presidential candidates would marry before the convention and would present themselves as couples for convention decision. Or, in the looser variant, each presidential contender would make public, in the preconvention period, a short list of his alternate marriage partners. But the calculations shaping such tickets would aim primarily at increasing convention support by fellow partisans, which is not necessarily the same thing as increasing the election appeal of the ticket to the general citizenry. Indeed, the strategy useful for the one may impede achievement of the other. For example, the policies that made Goldwater in 1964 and McGovern in 1972 popular to party delegates in convention later repelled more voters than they attracted at election time. When compelled to link up with a running mate early on, well before his convention strength can be reliably estimated, a presidential aspirant frequently would be under pressure to gain the backing of another policy faction. He might, therefore, select his running mate and compromise his policy views in accord with that need. And once he was locked into a particular ticket, he would find it difficult to maneuver or adjust in light of changing realities in the preconvention period. Under current practices, in contrast, the design of the ticket by the presidential candidate is ordinarily shaped by the quest for victory in the election to come.

In sum, the proposals in set 1 and set 2 to provide different preconvention nominating devices for the vice-presidency are grossly defective. Most would not serve their own intent, which is to upgrade the quality of vice-presidential nominees, because they would exclude presidential aspirants from consideration for the second spot. Some might achieve the objective sought, but at the high cost of excessively diluting or denying the presidential candidate's proper role in selecting his running mate and of often supplying a policy opponent of the presidential nominee as his ticket affiliate. The surest promise of these reforms, therefore, would be to handicap effective presidential candidacies, to hobble party campaign and election efforts, and to supply as a successor a vice-president with policy views dissimilar to those of the president.

CONVENTION NOMINATING CHANGES

Another set of reforms proposes changes in vice-presidential nominating procedures at the convention only, otherwise leaving intact the essentials of the present convention system and not requiring the introduction of preconvention vice-presidential primaries. Of the four proposals of this type to be discussed, three seek to deny the presidential candidate any role in designating his running mate, and the other would confine his choice to a restricted pool of possibilities. Almost certainly none would work out as intended and, in any event, their negative side effects would be more damaging by far than the limited benefits they might produce.

Two familiar proposals: The changes suggested by two of the proposals are much the same as those advanced in some of the preconvention reforms just reviewed, and they merit the same adverse judgment for much the same reasons. One such change calls for the automatic award of the vice-presidential nomination to the second-running candidate in the convention balloting for the presidential nomination. This would assure a high-quality vice-president and successorship—assuming, of course, the runner-up was willing to accept the nomination —but at the probable price of an unbalanced ticket composed of leaders of differing factions with divergent policy outlooks. Moreover, recourse to such a formula of selection would deprive not merely the head of the ticket but everyone of discretion and capacity to choose in light of circumstances and needs. There are times, obviously, when selecting the major losing presidential rival as the running mate makes strategic sense, but that does not justify mandating it as an inflexible rule that must be followed at all times. Current practice, in contrast, permits this outcome if the presidential nominee wishes, but does not require it regardless of his or anyone else's wishes.

The second of the two familiar changes would reverse the present sequence and schedule the convention's nomination of the vice-president before that of the president. This suffers from a variety of basic defects discussed in the preceding section, not the least of which is counterproductiveness in terms of its own purpose. The reform is intended to heighten the quality of vice-presidential nominees by focusing attention on the nomination in its own right and by taking the nomination out from under control by the presidential nominee. What it would accomplish in this regard, however, is to make high-quality leaders unavailable as a running mate, because they would have to sacrifice first-spot ambitions and chances to accept consideration for the second place on the ticket.

Neither of the two proposals, it should be noted, would likely succeed in insulating vice-presidential choice from the presidential nominee. On the first plan, a leading presidential contender who had delegate support well above the size needed for his nomination could instruct the transfer of some of his backing to a presidential rival he wished to have as his running mate. The effect of the proposal in such circumstances would be to define the pool of eligibles narrowly, but not to eliminate altogether the presidential nominee's ability to make the choice within that pool. On the second proposal, the odds are very high that the convention contest for the vice-presidential slot would become embroiled in the rivalry of presidential challengers, which would drain that contest of any substantive meaning it otherwise might have. As a consequence, the status of the vice-president would scarcely be enhanced even as the formation of the national ticket was forced prematurely.

An "open convention": A third suggestion, which in theory is also designed to prevent the presidential nominee from naming his ticket affiliate, would mandate an "open convention." This would establish as a new norm a hands-off policy by the party's standard-bearer, who would leave the decision on his running mate up to the convention delegates. In recent history, the only instance of this was the 1956 Democratic convention, when Adlai Stevenson was nominated for the second time to lose overwhelmingly to Eisenhower. Stevenson's neutrality on the vice-presidential nomination provoked a bitter convention fight between the supporters of Senator Estes Kefauver and Senator John F. Kennedy, which the former won. In 1972, McGovern sought to convey the impression of an "open convention," but there was never any doubt that his candidate, Senator Thomas F. Eagleton, would win handily.[18] McGovern tolerated delegate presentation of seven nominees and their voting for an even larger number, including Walter Cronkite, the television news

[18] In summer 1974, President Ford spoke of an "open convention" with respect to the vice-presidential nomination at the Republican 1976 convention. Understood in context, however, his remarks meant only that he was not prepared then to endorse continuation of incumbent Nelson Rockefeller, but that it would be his decision, not the convention's, whether to do so. Further, if Ford were to decide to let Rockefeller go, his replacement would also be up to Ford and would not be left to the delegates to determine. Ford's effort to keep his distance from Rockefeller was seen as a strategy to placate Republican conservatives, who at the time were considering supporting former Governor Ronald Reagan of California against Ford at the 1976 convention or as a third party in the 1976 election. In November 1975, when Rockefeller announced he was not interested in continuing as vice-president after the close of his term, it was widely held to mean that President Ford had judged him to be, on balance, a political liability with respect to Republican support and that the president was unwilling to select him as his running mate in 1976.

commentator, and Archie Bunker, the blue-collar
bigot in a highly popular television series.[19]

If this proposal led to a genuine "open convention," its only certain result would be to isolate the
head of the ticket from influencing who his running
mate would be, which would explicitly repudiate the
third key constraint discussed earlier. What it would
otherwise accomplish remains unclear. What other
forces would come to exercise control in place of the
standard-bearer? What intraparty divisiveness
might be stimulated, and with what effects on the
party's election prospects? What kinds of nominees
would be produced, and with what consequences for
the campaign, the vice-presidency, and successorship? The proposal would appear, on balance, to
entail serious costs without offsetting assurance of
significant benefits.

Most likely, however, an "open convention"
would turn out to be a sham because the presidential
nominee would choose or be compelled to attempt
to control the decision. Once that happened, presumably the delegates would continue their practice
of accommodating his decision. If gutting the reform openly were deemed impolitic, neither the
presidential nominee nor the convention delegates
would find it difficult to maintain its form nominal-

[19] The proceedings came across to many viewers less as
good fun or therapy for the delegates than as a questionable
exhibition on the edge of being a shambles. The antics so
protracted the session that McGovern had to delay his acceptance speech until 2:45 A.M. (Eastern Standard Time)—
hardly within prime viewing time!

ly while stripping it of its substance. It is possible, though unlikely, that delegates might use the principle of an "open convention" to dispute the ticket head's decision. Were that to occur, or were the presidential nominee to fail in getting convention endorsement of his selection, he would be forced to begin his campaign under the highly disadvantageous conditions of a public display of a seriously divided party and of his own ineffective leadership and influence. Neither of these outcomes says much in support of this proposed reform.

Defining eligibility: The final reform of this group to be considered goes in a direction different from the previous three. It fully maintains the ticket head's capacity to pick his partner but would limit his choice to those who had been placed in nomination for the presidency at the convention. If the most optimistic or "best case" expectations of the advocates of this proposal were likely to be met in practice, this reform might well be judged feasible. But a less sanguine prognosis is called for because of the reform's vulnerability to strategic misuse, which in turn argues for its undesirability and rejection.

The proposed rule would clearly invite extensive manipulation. It sets as a condition of eligibility for the second spot prior membership in the ranks of presidential entrants. That is an easy condition to fulfill. Every presidential aspirant could arrange to have the name of the person(s) he wished to consider as a running mate entered in the presidential balloting. And every would-be vice-presidential nominee could do the same; indeed, anyone who wanted not to exclude himself from that possibility would have to do the same in order to be eligible under the rule. The result would be, on the one side, to complicate, clutter, and cheapen the presidential contest, and, on the other, to negate the purpose of the reform because having been a presidential entrant would no longer serve as even a rough measure of high-quality standing or of possession of a "claim" on the vice-presidency.

This manipulation of the rule could be countered by amending it to set a minimum level of convention support in the presidential contest, whether by percentage of total vote or state distribution, to make one eligible for consideration for the vice-presidential spot. But the higher the minimum, the narrower the choice left to the presidential nominee. When so amended, the proposal would become but a slightly softer version of the earlier-rejected plan to assign the vice-presidential nomination to the runner-up presidential rival. (In situations of a two-man contest, however, the two reforms would operate identically.) As the intent of the amended proposal would be best met if a presidential competitor with sizable convention backing were tapped for the second place on the ticket, it would be relevant to speculate what might have happened at some conventions had this plan been in effect at the time. (What would have happened cannot be confidently determined because candidate strategy and delegate behavior might well have changed had such a nomination rule been in effect.)

On the Republican side, it could have led to the

vice-presidential nominee being General Douglas MacArthur in 1944, Robert Taft in 1952, and Barry Goldwater in 1960; for the Democrats, Al Smith in 1932, Senator Harry Byrd of Virginia in 1944, and Senator Richard Russell of Georgia in 1948. It will be noted that the securing of significant convention minority support is often associated with sectional and/or ideological dissidents. The proposal under examination would serve, however unintendedly, to build that dissidence right into the ticket and the vice-presidency itself.

Implications

The previous chapter concluded that the American political system was uncongenial to making regular use of the vice-presidency or any other office to establish a routine provision of presidential successorship of presumed presidential quality. Enduring systemic constraints have channeled the vice-presidency into serving other needs held more critical. This chapter, in effect, has grounded that conclusion in a review of numerous proposals which stubbornly insist on trying to revamp the vice-presidency to enable it to satisfy the need for high-quality successorship. Inescapably, then, these reforms consciously or implicitly do battle with the systemic constraints that have shaped that office to date. And because these reform proposals would and/or should lose that battle, they have here been judged undesirable. In their severe conflict with key constraints many of the reforms would have unanticipated effects which run so opposite to their intent as to aggravate the very problems they hoped to solve—for example, the self-defeating effort to supply high-quality presidential successors by settling the vice-presidential nomination before and in isolation from the presidential nomination contest. Some of the reforms would likely achieve what they sought, but only at the cost of neglect or harm to other compelling needs and values—for example, assigning the vice-presidential nomination to the runner-up presidential rival.

Two core conclusions thus emerge from the analysis to this point. If the problem of presidential succession is defined as the need to institutionalize provision of presidential-quality successors, the vice-presidency cannot be made or made over to meet that need on a routine basis without unduly dissatisfying other compelling needs of the political system. To meet this succession need in an acceptable fashion, the idea of a successorship office should be abandoned and that of a special presidential election introduced in its place. A special election would result, by definition, in the balance of the vacated presidential term being completed by a person of presidential quality. It would also satisfy, in the most direct and uncomplicated way, the claims of popular sovereignty as applied to the highest office in the land.

5

Key Constraints Honored: Feasible Reforms of the Vice-Presidency

It follows from the two core conlcusions just presented that if retention of the vice-presidency rested on its capacity to attract and house successors of presidential caliber, the office would warrant abolition. Yet the agenda of this chapter is to continue to review other reform proposals intended to improve the vice-presidential nominating process and the quality of vice-presidents. These proposals are based on an alternative formulation of the succession problem, one noted at the outset of this study and touched on again toward the close of the third chapter. It is entirely consonant with this new perspective to decide that the vice-presidency should be kept and that acceptable ways of strengthening its successorship function should be sought. In keeping with the analytical frame of this book, it is considered a necessary condition that an acceptable reform not conflict with key systemic constraints. It should not surprise, therefore, that those reforms found to qualify involve essentially modest change.

Another Formulation of the Problem

In many other countries, severe problems of political succession persist, in some cases chronically promoting instability of the basic regime. In America, by contrast, we have been able to operate by rapid and legitimated succession, even under such trying circumstances as assassination or incipient impeachment of the president. No small virtue of the present system, it should not be taken for granted as a practice easily developed or maintained or assured to Americans no matter what. Political succession arrangements, in short, lie close to the heart of political systems, are often fragile, and require constant care.

This view leads one to identify as the central concern of successorship America's capacity to handle swiftly and peacefully the problem of a vacated presidency. Successorship as the stable transfer of presidential power and successorship as a quest for presidential-quality successors are not necessarily complementary objectives. Of course, everyone's personal preference would be for better-quality rather than mediocre successors. But those committed to quick and stable succession as the highest priority would give only secondary concern to securing successors of the highest quality. That unconcern might change to hostility, however, if a special election were required to produce a presidential-quality successor. The risks of destabilization of the political system, in this view, would far outweigh the gains. A trade-off must be had, in other words, between protecting regime stability in potentially perilous circumstances like a vacated presidency and securing presidential-caliber successors through special election. It might be more prudent to have an unambiguous queue of specified successors, none of whom would be certain or perhaps even likely to be of presumed presidential quality, than to set in motion nomination and election contests of presidential-quality rivals.

This alternative formulation is by far the more modest of the two, requiring only that the succession process be rapid and stable, and that it produce someone considered legitimate and acceptable by the citizenry. Adoption of this definition of the problem leads to setting a fixed sequence of automatic succession, that is, by determining an ordered list of successorship offices. In that context, there would seem to be no a priori reason to promote some other office in place of the vice-presidency to the head of the succession line. For all the disabilities of the post, it always has been given first claim on successorship and, as it has turned out, only vice-presidents have ever succeeded to a vacated presidency. Those instances of succession generally have been accomplished rapidly and have been accepted by the public as legitimate. Moreover, and no less important, there does not appear to be any other high office which would likely do a predictably

better job on successorship or which has an obviously superior initial claim to successorship.

In undertaking a review of additional proposals to
improve the vice-presidency we may have some
confidence, therefore, that it does not unwittingly
lead to a neglect of alternative offices with greater
suitability or potential. In the review that follows,
reforms that are consistent with key systemic constraints are considered to be "feasible." Although a
reform must be feasible to be judged desirable, a
feasible reform may be either desirable or undesirable, depending on other factors.

Sharing in and/or Extending the Time for the Nomination Decision

In a description best characterized as a caricature
sufficiently close to the mark to be only an over-
statement, columnist Tom Wicker identifies some
major deficiencies in the way many nonincumbent
presidential nominees of the modern period have
come to their decision on their running mate:

> ... in a few hours of hasty consultation or as the result of
> earlier promises or dealings, [presidential nominees]
> produce their vice-presidential nominees from the hat,
> as it were. The latter are almost always chosen for
> political reasons, with virtually no investigation or study,
> and often with the public's having almost no concept of
> their qualities.[20]

[20] "A Ford for the Future?," *New York Times,* 14 October
1973.

Moderate proposals to remedy these deficiencies move in either or both of two directions. One is to require the head of the ticket to share with a party mechanism the decision-making on the vice-presidential nomination. The other is to extend the time available to make that nomination, which would relieve the currently frenetic pace of decision-making. Either route aims essentially at the same destination, namely, to provide a structure supportive of a fuller canvass of the field, a more deliberate review of the leading alternatives, and greater assurance of input from a variety of party sources. To the extent that none of these proposals would actually deny the presidential nominee the controlling say in designating his ticket affiliate, all merit consideration as feasible reforms. Their desirability, however, is more variable, as the following review seeks to make clear.

CONVENTION CHOICE FROM AMONG NAMES SUBMITTED BY PRESIDENTIAL NOMINEE

One suggestion for decision-sharing would have the party's newly selected ticket head submit to the convention a list of three persons acceptable to him as a running mate, and then the convention would make its own choice among them.[21] Although its

[21] In Chapter 4, a comparable proposal, but one applied to all presidential aspirants in the preconvention period, was deemed undesirable. The reform now under discussion is free from the major defects of the other, which were to force premature ticket construction and to require persons to declare for vice-presidential candidacy before the presidential nomination was determined.

intent is clear, this procedure might stimulate more
varied and unpredictable response than its propo-
nents anticipate. One likely pattern of reaction
would make the reform more cosmetic than substantive, and of a kind not necessarily producing an
improved appearance. Under present practices, although the presidential nominee's mode of consultation and decision-sharing varies according to his
inclinations and circumstances, he is assigned and
he accepts an open responsibility for the naming of
his running mate. The procedure under examination, however, may often move the standard-bearer,
not toward a wider involvement of others in the
making of the decision, but toward exercising his
own control more covertly and without being held
as clearly responsible for the outcome.

It seems quite naive, after all, to assume that the
presidential nominee would be truly indifferent to
which of the trio of persons he has offered gets the
convention's nod—or to the extent of bruising
intraparty fighting his list of three might provoke.
A more reasonable expectation is that the list would
be designed to promote convention support for the
standard-bearer's preference and to minimize party
division in the convention. Typically, the convention would endorse the presidential nominee's
choice, as is the case under present procedures. But
as the proposal calls, in form, for convention determination in the context of nonintervention by the
presidential nominee, stratagems and deceits would
come to be more heavily relied on to achieve the
same end. Few would be fooled by such transparent

dodges, of course, and hence the change, if it operated as here described, would serve mostly to increase public cynicism about the convention system.

Further, it would be hard to overstate the practical difficulties and high political risks involved in
conforming to this new procedure. From the viewpoint of a prospective vice-presidential nominee, it
is one thing to be considered among others privately
by the presidential nominee and his associates, but it
is quite a different matter to be asked to compete
publicly for the position in a three-person contest in
which only one can win. From the viewpoint of the
presidential nominee, the obligation to name three
as possibilities rather than one as his nominee may
put him in the politically awkward position of
seeming to exclude as unacceptable to him a much
longer list of others, many of whom might resent
the exclusion on personal or factional grounds. Such
tensions would place the ticket leader in a strategic
dilemma. Finally, from the viewpoint of convention
delegates, what is supposed to guide their choice
among the trio put before them if the presidential
nominee does not intervene futher? And in what
respects, if any, might one expect their decision to
be any wiser, more strategic, or otherwise superior
to that of the standard-bearer?

PARTY COMMITTEE RECOMMENDATION, CONVENTION CHOICE

In another proposal, a special committee chaired by
the presidential nominee but composed of party
leaders designated by the National Committee and

of representatives of significant presidential contenders defeated at the convention would meet to
agree on a vice-presidential nominee to recommend
to the convention. If disagreement obtained, the
presidential nominee's preference and the committee's plurality or majority preference would be reported to the convention, which would make the
final decision. This reform leaves unclear how such
a committee should or would function, but its intent
is to force on the presidential nominee a process of
party and factional consultation which, at the least,
would require him to justify his choice of running
mate to a broad range of influential party leaders
and, on occasion, might lead to a genuine sharing of
decision as to who would best fill the second place on
the ticket.

This proposal is constructive in purpose but
wrongly seeks to formalize what should remain
informal. Other things being equal, it is better for a
presidential nominee to touch many party bases as
part of his coming to a decision on his running mate.
But the hard truth is that unless party leadership or
the convention is willing to cripple the campaign
and fragment party support, there is no effective
way to deny the presidential nominee the vice-
presidential affiliate he strongly wants. Hence burdening the leader of the ticket with having to move
his choice through the ill-defined committee suggested by this proposal is not likely to change the
outcome, but merely to give it a worse appearance
and less legitimacy. The process, after all, seems

closer to the smoke-filled room than to a public exercise of shared power.

PRESERVING THE CONVENTION'S ROLE?

An evaluation of reforms which enlarge the time period for nominating a running mate requires one to judge whether convention participation in the nominating process must continue to be assured. It is instructive to note that all the diverse proposals examined thus far in this study retain the convention's authority—whether deemed nominal or real—to make the vice-presidential nomination. There is much to be said for that position. Our national parties become national largely in connection with the quadrennial presidential contest, and the several thousands of delegates who come together in the nominating convention constitute the parties' supreme authority and exercise its most critical functions. The convention is the proper and best arena in which to conduct the brokerage, bargaining, and reconciling activities characteristic of our decentralized party system. If, therefore, the nomination of the vice-president is considered an important party function, it would be most appropriate for the convention, rather than some other party agency, to perform it.

If retention of a convention role is held to as a high-priority constraint, only the most modest change at the margin becomes possible. Its purpose would be to provide more time than is presently available—less than twenty-four hours—between the convention's decision on who the presidential candidate will be and the latter's decision on who the vice-presidential nominee will be. That extra time could be used to improve the quality of consideration given to the roster of possibilities, to promote input by and consultation with party leaders, to permit a more thorough checking out of the background of the intended nominee, and the like.

But the extra time that could be made available is of the order of another day or two at the most, secured by revising the convention's schedule of events. At present, the party platform is adopted on the second day, the presidential nomination is made on the third day, and the vice-presidential nomination on the fourth and final day. An extra day's time could be had by nominating the president before adopting the platform, but this would raise serious substantive and strategic questions relating to the presidential nomination. More simply, a fifth day could be added, on which the vice-presidential nomination would occur. Even so brief an extension of time would help to relieve the currently breakneck pace of decision-making on the vice-presidency, but it could not realistically be expected to accomplish much more than that.

There is no way, consequently, to reconcile the convention's short time-frame with the kind of considered and careful filling of the vice-presidential spot that reformers stress as a necessary improvement. Significantly more time for the nomination decision can be had only by moving the matter into the postconvention period and by depriving the convention of any direct involvement in its settle-ment. Whether such a trade-off is worth it remains open to considerable disagreement.

POSTCONVENTION DETERMINATION

The reform proposals of those who believe in the value of that trade-off typically seek to substitute another party mechanism for the exclusion of the convention and to give party legitimacy to the nomination. The suggestions cover a gamut by now all too familiar to the reader. One proposes a vice-presidential national primary, with plurality winner. Another would have the presidential nom-inee submit his preference to the National Commit-tee, which would vote it up or down. Still another would vary that plan, by calling for the submission of a list of three or four acceptable names, from which the committee would make its choice. (Note that the representativeness of a postconvention National Committee would likely be considered acceptable, for its members would have been newly selected.) A more cumbersome proposal would es-tablish some sort of special party committee, includ-ing the presidential nominee, party leaders, and representatives of the major defeated presidential aspirants, which would recommend a name for confirmation by the National Committee. If dead-lock occurred or several names were forthcoming, the National Committee would be empowered to make the choice. The voting strength of each state's members on the National Committee could be weighted to mirror state delegation strength at the recently concluded convention.

A reminder on the salient criteria to apply, rather than a detailed review of each suggestion, should suffice for appraisal. An acceptable postconvention mechanism should maintain the presidential candidate's ultimate control of the choice. It should provide for a short interval of time—say, no longer than seven to ten days after the close of the convention—and avoid either a lengthy or an open-ended time period. It should eschew creating a procedure which appears to provide greater democracy but actually operates otherwise. If, then, one of the proposals just set forth had to be adopted, the most tolerable would be submission of the presidential candidate's choice to the National Committee. The committee, it should be emphasized, would be expected to perform a symbolic role of party legitimation by routinely confirming the choice, not to dispute the decision-making power of the head of the ticket or to convert it into a collegial authority.[22]

[22] The line of analysis here undertaken fits nicely with the modesty of the recommendations put forth by the Democratic National Committee's Special Commission on Vice-Presidential Selection, which was formed as a consequence of Senator George McGovern's difficulties in securing a running mate in 1972. The commission proposed adoption of either of two marginal changes: calendar rearrangement and adding a day to the convention *or* moving the decision to the postconvention period by having the presidential nominee submit one or more names to the Democratic National Committee. These recommendations were not acted on, and many felt the commission had labored mightily only to bring forth a "mouse." Yet if this book's analysis is sound, that disdainful

Two other possibilities merit brief discussion. It would give both the presidential nominee and the convention greater flexibility if the option were available of settling the vice-presidential nomination either at the convention or at the postconvention stage. The initiative would rest with the presidential nominee. If his needs were better met by rapid choice confirmed by the convention, he could submit his designee's name to the convention. If, on the other hand, a longer time period was preferred, he could inform the convention that the nomination would be made at a later date by whatever postconvention procedures the party had adopted. Providing a presidential nominee with such a choice, in contrast to locking him in to one or the other, would not only enlarge his discretion, however, but also would open him up to considerable pressures. Whether, on balance, more headache than help would likely result is arguable.

The other possibility is to authorize the presidential nominee to announce in the postconvention period—directly, on his own, and without even the gesture of confirmation by a party mechanism—his choice of his running mate. This proposal is likely to go against the grain for most people, even among those who clearly understand that the procedure would merely sanction what is often the reality as distinct from the appearance. The reaction might be different, perhaps, if at the end of the road the

---

response is but the most recent example of an enduring misperception of the frustrating problem of the vice-presidency.

customary election controls for an elective office were operative. But they are not, because we cannot vote on the vice-president separately from the president. Given that limitation, it is questionable whether the public would support a proposal which would strip the original nomination of any appearance of having been a broadly-based party decision and openly acknowledge it as the decision of a single person, the presidential nominee.

An Appointive Vice-Presidency?

The broad logic behind the last proposal—post-convention unilateral determination by the presidential nominee—is to match form to substance. That logic can be taken a step further to propose changing a basic attribute of the vice-presidency in a way not yet explored in this study in spite of the plethora of reforms already discussed, namely, conversion of the post from an elective to an appointive one. Such a possibility would have fallen on deaf ears in the pre-Twenty-fifth Amendment period, when the reality was that either the office was occupied by the initially elected vice-president or it was vacant and left unfilled. However, now that we have recently experienced the appointment of two vice-presidents, there should be an increased willingness to review such a plan genuinely and seriously. The lengthiness of the review that follows reflects the need to examine a new and significantly different proposal fully, especially because it has not been subjected as yet to much critical assessment. The reader should not misinterpret this extensive attention as any indicator of the writer's preferred solution. An appointive vice-presidency does pass muster by the analytic criteria here employed, and hence it is considered to be a feasible reform. But whether it is a desirable reform or, more grandly, the best of the feasible alternatives here presented, is up to each reader for individual determination.

In conducting this review, there is no point in diffusing discussion by multiplying nomination and confirmation alternatives for consideration. Realistically, and in keeping with systemic constraints, the appointment procedure that warrants our full attention is nomination by the president and confirmation by the Congress. To propose an appointive vice-presidency, then, is in effect to propose that sections 1 and 2 of the Twenty-fifth Amendment become standard operating procedure for filling the position initially as well as when it is vacated prematurely. A new constitutional amendment would be necessary, of course, to provide for election of only the president and to stipulate the appointment process for the vice-president, including resolution of some important problems on timing and on further procedures in the event of congressional rejection of the nominee.[23]

[23] As alternate acceptable solutions to these problems exist, dissection of them is not necessary for the main concerns of the analysis. On the problem of timing, for example, it might be preferable to set the nomination-and-confirmation process for the period from the Electoral

CONSIDERING THE CONCEPT

The proposal for an appointive vice-presidency emerged in late 1973 in reaction to the two "catastrophes" that had recently beset the vice-presidency. The first was the forced withdrawal of Senator Thomas F. Eagleton (Democrat, Missouri) as McGovern's running mate in 1972, when, shortly after his nomination, it became known that he had earlier in his life received shock treatment for a nervous disorder. The second was the forced resignation in 1973 of Vice President Spiro Agnew, formerly governor of Maryland and Baltimore County Executive, for illegal monies taken from Maryland contractors before and during his first term. Neither Eagleton nor Agnew had been well known at the time of his nomination, and the designation of each had come about in typically hurried fashion. In seeking to learn from those episodes, one might choose to conclude that an Eagleton-type problem could be averted in the future by lengthening the time period for decision, but not an Agnew-type problem. Not even Agnew's need to conduct a campaign for elective office, against competition which had every incentive to

College's confirmation of the presidential victor in December to Inauguration Day in January. If that would give the new Congress insufficient time, a later deadline could be set, with contingency successorship to operate should the presidency become vacant before the vice-presidential nominee was confirmed. On the problem of congressional turndown of the nominee, provision could be made for successive nominations, with a time limit in each case for congressional action.

review his background closely, had provided an adequate safeguard. Perhaps, then, it would be better to have the vice-presidency occupied by someone nominated by the president and closely reviewed for confirmation by the Congress, on the model of what was then occurring on Nixon's nomination of Gerald Ford to the vice-presidency?

A less auspicious period for promoting support of this novel idea could scarcely be imagined. Its sponsor, Senator Robert Griffin (Republican, Michigan), had come to it in reaction to one set of events and concerns, but another set quickly emerged to occupy center stage. Griffin's proposal was preoccupied with the vice-presidency, but the deepening Watergate pall shifted the spotlight to the presidency. Whereas Griffin's plan called for the presidential nomination and congressional confirmation of all vice-presidents in order to improve their quality, others were questioning the wisdom of that procedure when applied to filling a vacated vice-presidency, as provided by section 2 of the Twenty-fifth Amendment. Their Watergate-induced perspective on the problem led them to ask, of course, whether an increasingly discredited president should have the right to name the person who might well have to complete his own presidential term. "There is something troubling," observed Senator William D. Hathaway (Democrat, Maine), "about a president who is under threat of impeachment or forced resignation having the power to name his successor."[24] Others called the same

[24] *New York Times,* 9 November 1973.

thought "preposterous" and "a total howling political absurdity."[25] When that succession took place in August 1974, additional questions were raised about the wisdom of permitting appointed vice-presidents to fill a presidential vacancy, as provided in section 1 of the Twenty-fifth Amendment.

Although sparked by the atypical events of Nixon's besieged and truncated second term, opposition to the idea of appointing the vice-president or the successor to a vacated vice-presidency obviously has deeper roots. Two separate but usually intertwined criteria are often advanced. One is that a president's control over successorship as direct as his appointment of his successor is repugnant to a democracy, and should not be allowed. The other is that presidential successorship posts should be elective, not appointive. If valid, these positions would dispose of the proposal promptly and negatively, and hence they call for careful comment.

When applied to the vice-presidency as the first successor to a vacated presidency, these criteria sharply distinguish between elective (pass) and appointive (fail) versions. But is this discrimination justified? In both versions, after all, presidential control is predominant, and it must be exercised in awareness of the confirmatory role of others. For the elective vice-president, the choice must not offend the convention, fellow partisans, or the

[25] The first quotation is from historian Arthur Schlesinger, Jr. *(New York Times,* 27 February 1975); the second from law professor Charles L. Black, Jr. *(New York Times,* 20 December 1974).

public, and for the appointive vice-presidency, not the Congress, fellow partisans, or the public. Most critically, the elective vice-president comes to his office less through winning his own election in any meaningful sense than by piggy-backing on the presidential winner in the contest that has truly engaged the nation and on which the only real electoral decision has been made. From the standpoint of popular sovereignty, then, neither the elected nor the appointed vice-president links directly to the voters; both make connection indirectly through the president who selected them and whom the voters elected. It follows that efforts to deny a vice-president who is appointed to his full term of office the same direct successorship role granted to an elected vice-president mistakenly confuse major differences in form with minor differences in substance.

Regardless of whether the original vice-president is elected (Twenty-fifth Amendment) or appointed (the proposal under discussion), should the appointed successor to a vacated vice-presidency be permitted to succeed to a vacated presidency? Applying the position just developed, the decision should turn on whether the presidential nominator does or does not connect to popular sovereignty through his own election as president. If a successor vice-president is nominated by an elected president, he should be able to succeed to a vacated presidency in the same way (and for the same reasons) as the original vice-president. The situation is quite different, however, for a successor president, whether he was formerly an elected or appointed vice-president. His appointee as vice-president should not be allowed to succeed to a vacated presidency, because the appointee's relationship to the original president and presidential election would be too attenuated to square with popular sovereignty and democratic legitimacy.[26] Assuming that a vacated vice-presidency would always be filled rather than left vacant, the rule may be restated in shorthand fashion: within a regular four-year term, only one succession to a vacated presidency but multiple successions to a vacated vice-presidency should be allowed.

For example, this rule would endorse the appropriateness of Vice-President Ford's succession to the presidency, but it would deny to Vice-President Rockefeller the right to succeed to the presidency if Ford were unable to complete his term. Another contingency successorship arrangement must be provided, therefore, for this category of double vacancy in which the successor president is also prevented from finishing the original term of office and the vice-president, being himself a successor, is not entitled to become president. (In the other category of double vacancy, the position under discussion, like the Twenty-fifth Amendment, permits a successor vice-president to succeed to a presidency

---

[26] This position is fundamentally similar to President Truman's strongly held view that a successor president should not be able to name his successor. That view was implemented, at a pre-Twenty-fifth Amendment time when a vacated vice-presidency stayed unfilled, by moving first contingent successorship from the Cabinet to the congressional leadership.

vacated by the elected president.) In such circumstances either type of succession arrangement—special election or successorship by the House Speaker—could be strongly argued. Perhaps the decision should be made by a coin toss, if only on the statistical grounds of the extraordinary odds against the occurrence of a situation in which two presidents were unable to complete the same term and a sizable balance of the term still remained.

How did the idea of an appointive vice-president come to be included in the Twenty-fifth Amendment, and how does its rationale there relate to the concept as developed here? Taken in its own mid-sixties setting, the problem was not seen as a choice between an elective or appointive vice-president, much less as one between an elected or nonelected president. It was seen, rather, as choosing between alternate contingent successors, with no serious consideration given to the special election device and with the expectation that a double vacancy would not arise in the future, just as it had not in the past, and hence that contingent successorship would never really come into play. Everyone agreed the elected vice-president should remain the direct successor, but what contingent successorship should there be if the vice-presidency was vacant?[27] The choice, in effect, was to assign first contingent succession to the top congressional leadership or the

[27] Through 1967, there had been sixteen vacancies in the vice-presidency, totaling thirty-seven years, occasioned by seven deaths, one resignation, and eight successions to a vacant presidency.

Cabinet heads on the one side, or to "another" vice-president on the other. Congress opted for the latter, and then chose presidential nomination and congressional confirmation in preference to a special election as the mode of selecting a successor vice-president.[28] The elected vice-president was thus the direct successor, the appointed vice-president was the first contingent successor, and both had the same right to succeed to a vacated presidency.

The rationale of sections 1 and 2 of the Twenty-fifth Amendment thus lends no real support to the concept of an appointive vice-presidency. All it does is to prefer as the primary contingent successor an appointed vice-president instead of the Speaker of the House or the secretary of state. On the other hand, it implicitly reaffirms election and rejects appointment as the mode of selection of the initial vice-president in any administration. Most basically, the amendment reflects no theoretical concern at all with the concept of either an appointive or an elective vice-presidency. That deficiency is neither a small nor an academic matter because it probably was this neglect, rather than the excusable inability of the sponsors to predict future events, that accounts for their failure to limit the cycle of successorship to a vacated presidency to one full turn, as suggested here. Both the Twenty-fifth Amendment

---

[28] At no time in our history has there been any significant support for the idea of holding a special election to fill a vacated vice-presidency. That judgment would appear to be sound.

and the broader proposal under discussion should be amended, then, to allow only those vice-presidents who were appointed by the elected president to complete an interrupted presidency.

OPERATION AND EFFECTS

To be considered a desirable reform, an appointive vice-presidency must operate in practice in ways consistent with major systemic constraints and with high promise of improving the quality of vice-presidents. The key questions for inquiry relate to the probable behavior of the president (what kinds of nominees?) and of Congress (what criteria for confirmation?), and to their mutual relationship (nomination type affects confirmation criteria, and vice versa). Assessment of these matters cannot escape being speculative in good part, but advantage can be taken of the limited experience made available by the two recent exercises of section 2 of the Twenty-fifth Amendment in filling a vacated vice-presidency.

The behavior of Congress in reviewing and confirming the appointments of Ford (1973) and Rockefeller (1974) as vice-president was quite consistent with what is appropriate, indeed with what is necessary, for the effective operation of that appointment process. The president's authority to nominate was not viewed as one in which Congress was entitled to share but rather as a unilateral presidential appointment subject to congressional confirmation. In exercising its confirmation author-

ity, Congress showed no signs of confusing its role
with the quite different one possessed by the people
in an election. It implicitly assumed that the nominee would be of the president's party, even when
the Congress was controlled by the opposition
party.[29] It behaved in no way to suggest that the
price of its confirmation would be to insist on a
particular nominee or to impinge on the separation
of powers by intruding on the president's right to
make his own selection.[30] Finally, and most critically, Congress seemed disposed to confirm the president's choice, as long as the nominee's personal and

[29] It has been suggested with reference to both the
Twenty-fifth Amendment and this proposal that a recon-
vened Electoral College should have the confirmation authority, not the Congress, in order to guarantee that an appointed
vice-president would be of the same party as the president.
But this would clearly give less legitimacy to the process and
to the appointee, especially if he were later to succeed to the
presidency, for such a confirmation would be *pro forma* and
entirely devoid of any review function. On this trade-off, it
makes more sense to rely on confirmation by Congress, which
can provide the requisite review of the nomination and can
maintain informal but effective constraints against partisan
abuse.

[30] These comments should not be misread as implying
presidential indifference to congressional reaction or automatic congressional support for any nominee the president
might choose to present. Speculation had it, for example,
that Nixon sounded out congressional sentiment on John B.
Connally, found it negative, and hence never offered his name
for vice-president. (Connally was a former governor of Texas
and secretary of treasury under Johnson, who had become an
adviser to Nixon and switched his party affiliation to the
Republicans in 1973. Resented by Democrats as a defector
and by Republicans as a Johnny-come-lately, Connally
aroused additional criticism as a possible vice-president be-

official probity checked out and there were no serious failings of character, temperament, or abilities that would disqualify him for the presidency, should he be called on to succeed to that post.[31]

The postconfirmation behavior of both Congress and the appointees has been similarly apt. Congress has not acted as if it had any special claim on Ford or Rockefeller, and neither of them, in turn, has shown any special sense of obligation to the legislature that confirmed their nomination.[32] Overall, then, Congress effectively defined and applied its new authority to confirm presidential nominations to fill a vacated vice-presidency. One cannot be sure, be-

---

cause of his known presidential ambitions.) This example falls well within the give-and-take expected of an interactive presidential nomination-congressional confirmation process.

[31] For reasons not necessary to go into here, the margin of Congress's approval of Ford was greater than that of Rockefeller. Still, Rockefeller was confirmed by better than a two-to-one ratio in the House and with over 90 percent support in the Senate.

[32] For example, President Ford has not hesitated to veto or to threaten to veto legislation he disagrees with, and he has made frequent use of that power in dealing with a Democratic Congress. Yet that has not led to any issue being raised of a nonelected president balking an elected Congress. The following statement of New York's Governor Hugh Carey should be considered as the rare exception that proves the rule: "I am hopeful that a president who was not elected by the people will give very careful consideration as to whether he should override an action by representatives who have been elected by the people" (*San Francisco Chronicle*, 8 November 1975). The context for the comment was the effort by the Congress to come up with legislation that would enable New York City to avoid default, a strategy opposed by President Ford and which he had announced he would veto.

cause the context was the troubled Watergate
period, that solid precedents have been set, but it
seems reasonable to suppose that Congress would
behave as responsibly in more normal times and
when, as the proposal under discussion requires, it
had to review the nominee put forward by a duly
elected president at the outset of his term.

Some have criticized Congress's confirmation
hearings as having been too concentrated on the
nominee's life and activities from the viewpoint of
probity, and insufficiently concerned with his policy
record and outlook. Although post-Watergate sensi-
tivities doubtless intensified this focus, that general
balance (or imbalance) of emphasis is likely to be a
durable characteristic. On the one side, there are few
clear or unpartisan standards of "correct" policy,
and there is widespread acknowledgment of the
president's right to pick someone he expects will be
able to work in harmony with him. On the other
side, however, there is a clearer and less partisan
standard of what probity is and a widespread belief
that any nominee should have to demonstrate his
record is "clean" in this regard as a condition of
securing confirmation.

Other critics have termed it a "ludicrous double
standard" that a short-term appointed vice-president should be subjected to a closer scrutiny than the
full-term elected president. But justification for an
extensive congressional review rests on the appointive character of the office (as in Cabinet nominations) and on the unique importance of its presidential successorship role. Further, the proposal

under discussion would substitute appointment for election and for the full term, which imposes a special obligation on the Congress, as the sole check point, to undertake a comprehensive review. Clearly, the scrutiny involved in congressional review of a presidentially nominated vice-president would be more demanding than that of either elected vice-presidents or of the House Speaker or the secretary of state (viewed as contingent presidential successors).

The timetable built into the concept of an appointive vice-presidency is intended to strengthen the presidential nominee's hand by providing him with ample time to consider the possibilities and with the fullest flexibility and discretion as to whom he might choose. Not so occasionally, however, strategic necessities might push a presidential nominee to name his intended vice-president well in advance of the election. The party-unifying or ticket-strengthening needs served by present practice in the designation of the party's vice-presidential nominee would not be eliminated, after all, by formal deferral of decision time to the postelection period. Particularly in the case of an incumbent president running for reelection, it often might prove too awkward to hold off a public commitment on whether the incumbent vice-president would be reappointed. Or a presidential nominee running behind his rival in the opinion polls might choose to revitalize his campaign by a dramatic announcement on who his vice-president would be. And if one major-party presidential contestant stated his vice-presidential

intention in the preelection period, the other would
come under heavy pressure to do the same. The
strong possibility that the decision timetable on an
appointed vice-president might be sharply fore-
shortened in practice makes it all the more impera-
tive that Congress maintain a high quality of review
in its confirmation role.

How would appointed vice-presidents differ
from those elected under current arrangements?
The differences would be least, presumably, when
conditions led the presidential nominees to make
their designation early in the campaign, though the
major difference of having to pass the congressional
confirmation process would still remain. For purposes of the discussion that follows, it will be
assumed that the decision on the vice-presidency
would not be publicly made until after the election,
an assumption which results in accentuating the
presumed differences.

In determining his choice of nominee, assuming
he had not boxed himself in by a convention or
campaign commitment, the president could seek to
help his postelection need to provide effective
governmental leadership. Whether that would give
him more or less flexibility of choice than the
presidential nominee has under current procedures
would depend on the election circumstances and the
particular needs of the new president. Gaining office by a landslide victory, for example, might provide the incoming president with a very large range
of choice. If he had just squeaked into office, however, in part because of the desertion of some of his

party supporters, the new president might be tightly constrained by strategic necessities in whom he could nominate for vice-president. The difference would lie, then, not so much in the degree of flexibility of choice as in the criteria of choice: presidential nominees select their running mates for convention, campaign, and election purposes, with little thought to postelection concerns, whereas presidents could appoint their vice-presidents with their governance needs uppermost in mind.[33]

For reasons explored earlier in this book, the president would have no incentive to select a nominee in self-conscious satisfaction of the need for an "alternate president" in case presidential successorship was required.[34] He might wish to take advantage, however, of the fact that some highly qualified persons who would make effective public officials (including service as vice-president) could not hope to secure office through the nomination-and-election route but could be recruited through appointment. In that sense the president could have

[33] It is conceivable that a farsighted president might choose, at the outset of his first term, someone he estimated would strengthen his reelection chances four years later. Presumably such a choice would help his first-term governance needs as well, but that would not be his primary concern.

[34] If, as earlier speculated, President Ford nominated Rockefeller as vice-president in 1974 in part to eliminate him as a rival in 1976, at least this kind of incentive to select an "alternate president" should be noted. But an elected president—which Ford was not—ordinarily has no significant opposition in securing convention renomination for a second term, and hence it is a most uncharacteristic incentive.

more flexibility of choice, perhaps, than the presidential nominee has under the present rules. But, on the other side, the choice would have to be made with a close eye on the relative ease of confirmation. Some persons or categories of persons are likely to be able to secure quicker and more consensual congressional approval than others, which might result in ruling out some who would have comfortably made it by the election route. A president typically will have little incentive to start his term by nominating as vice-president someone who would provoke protracted hearings and extensive negative reaction initially, even if ultimate approval by the Congress could be counted on. Hence controversial appointments—operationally defined as those likely to stimulate sizable or intense adverse response in Congress—would likely be avoided. Further, the nominee would have to possess a "clean" record in all important respects, and to be willing to have that record subjected to thorough public exposure and close legislative scrutiny, no matter how respected the nominee or how well known his prior service.[35]

The greater a president's need for rapid, noncontroversial, and supportive reaction by Congress for his nominee, the greater the temptation might be for him to nominate one of Congress's own respected members. President Nixon, most anxious to

[35] For example, the congressional confirmation hearings on Rockefeller, who had been elected four times as governor of New York, uncovered for the first time his practice of providing and forgiving personal loans to a variety of persons, including some public officials in New York.

avoid any struggle with Congress over Agnew's successor, exploited that strategy in his nomination of Gerald Ford, a veteran legislator and Republican House leader. Selecting someone from his congressional party would also make available to the president an agent who could use his intimate knowledge of legislative operations and his working relationships with congressmen to promote the president's cause in Congress. Although President Ford did not go this road, choosing former Governor Rockefeller instead, he had reason to be confident of his own skills in relating to Congress. Ford's decision also suggests, however, a basis for surmising that appointed vice-presidents would not come disproportionately from the ranks of Congress. Presidents who themselves had a strong congressional background might well prefer to nominate someone with a different political base, and in recent decades major presidential aspirants, nominees, and winners have come mostly from a congressional rather than a gubernatorial background.

The difficulties of confident prediction on this subject are nicely underscored by noting how President John F. Kennedy's behavior deviated from expectations discussed here. Himself a senator, Kennedy nonetheless picked Lyndon B. Johnson, the Democratic Senate leader, as his running mate. But then, in spite of his deepening troubles with Congress over support for his programs, President Kennedy made no attempt to tap his vice-president's fabled skills as a legislative leader. It would seem fairest to conclude, therefore, that although some circumstances would encourage a president to choose a valued member of Congress as his nominee for vice-president, and other circumstances would lead him to look in a different direction, in neither case would he be genuinely constrained in his choice. The touchstone for his decision on who to nominate could and likely would remain the president's own definition of his most presssing governance needs. The ability of a president to retain and act on so large a discretion would rest, of course, on Congress's continued willingness to confirm any suitable nominee he proferred and not just those recruited from the Congress itself.

What does this projected behavior by presidents and Congresses add up to on the key question of the likely quality of appointed vice-presidents? In view of the long history of dashed hopes and reform disillusionment on the subject of improving the vice-presidency, a sobering note should be injected right at the outset. There is nothing built into the operation of an appointive vice-presidency which would prohibit or even discourage presidents from naming, in the manner of presidential nominees under the present system, politically safe, relatively obscure, and seemingly mediocre nominees. There is a strong basis for expecting the prior record and standing of appointed vice-presidents to be superior, on the average, to what has characterized our elected vice-presidents—but there can be no guarantee that that will, in fact, occur. Much would depend on the development of a tradition of selecting known and competent persons, and in this regard the "precedents" set by the appointments of Ford and Rockefeller are most helpful.

An expected rise in quality should not be confused, however, with an explicit search for an "alternate president," which systemic constraints would continue to discourage. In earlier discussion of the present system, the problem of vice-presidents of low or uneven quality was described here as follows: "Traditionally slighted [in deciding the vice-presidential nomination] has been consideration of who was most qualified to complete an unfinished presidential term and, all too often, of whether the person chosen to balance the ticket was even minimally qualified for successorship." Avoidance of the latter rather than achievement of the former constitutes a realistic estimate of this reform's probable effects.

Once in office, however, an appointed vice-president would be expected to function—or not to function—in about the same way elected vice-presidents have. The president's appointment of the vice-president would intensify the latter's role, already highly developed under present procedures, as his subordinate and agent. Lacking even the form of endorsement by the party convention or the electorate, the appointed vice-president would owe his incumbency entirely to the president. Congress's review and confirmation, while vital to making the appointment process legitimate, would be reactive and not initiatory, and hence Congress would have no rival claim on the vice-president. Although the vice-president would continue to serve a fixed term of office, and not be subject to dismissal by the president, he would operate within the executive branch only to the extent and in ways the president wished.[36] At best, then, changing to an appointive vice-president might upgrade the average quality of the incumbent (and hence of the direct presidential successor), but it would not bring about any redefinition of the constricted and dependent role of the vice-presidency in our political system.

[36] It is possible that as a presidentially appointed rather than an elected official, the vice-president might come to be treated by the president as if he served at the president's pleasure instead of having a set four-year term. Suppose, for example, the president became dissatisfied with the vice-president or felt a strong political need to put someone else in that post? Public and congressional resistance to presidentially induced turnover in the direct successorship post would be the best safeguard against this development, but perhaps it also might be wise to consider requiring congressional confirmation by extraordinary rather than simple majority vote. There still remains, however, the thorny problem of what should be done when a vice-president loses the confidence and backing of the president who nominated him in the first place.

6

Conclusion

In determining the best mechanism for presidential succession, the broad choice before us is between the vice-presidency, desirably improved, and a special presidential election. However, as a desirably improved vice-presidency could be either an elective or appointive office, in effect we have three options. Selecting among these options involves deciding between alternative definitions of the problem of succession, assessing the extent to which the vice-presidency could be altered without violating key systemic constraints, and estimating the probable effects of numerous specific proposals for change. The purpose of this concluding chapter, which briefly restates the main lines of analysis of the three options, is to facilitate the reader's decision on which option he or she prefers.

Either of two views of presidential succession leads to a preferment for a special presidential election in the event of a vacated presidency. One view holds to a literal, no-nonsense reading of the idea that the president "be elected" and of popular sovereignty, and interprets it to mean that the only legitimate incumbent is one who has been elected to be the president, not someone who was selected to be something else and then succeeded to the presidency. The other view involves an initial willingness to forego special presidential elections on condition that the succession process produce a successor of presumed presidential quality. Finding that condition unrealizable, partisans of this view ultimately turn to special elections as their solution.

The analysis in this book has sought to portray the how and why of the American political system's profound unreceptivity to the provision of "alternate presidents," whether located in the vice-presidency or elsewhere or in elective or appointive offices. Of the many proposed reforms of the vice-presidency we have examined, most would actually operate differently from or contrary to their intent, and only a few would make almost certain the assignment of the vice-presidential nomination and/or the vice-presidency to a leader of presidential caliber. And of those few, in every instance major systemic constraints would be undercut, meaning that the reforms, on balance, would be unfeasible and undesirable and, because of that, politically unadoptable as well. Thus, for example, political costs would far exceed benefits were the vice-presidential nomination awarded by rigid rule to the defeated presidential contender who had the second-highest convention vote. Hence persons who hold to the second view, stymied in their quest to assure presidential-quality succession by revision of the vice-presidency, must come to embrace the idea of special presidential elections. Some would do so reluctantly and others eagerly, some with trepidation and others with equanimity, but all would do so on the shared judgment that no more moderate option came close enough to solving the problem of succession as they had defined it.

What is the impact of this judgment on the question of retention of the vice-presidency? With special presidential elections there is need for interim or provisional successorship, that is, an acting president for a brief period. Opinion is likely to be divided, with one group willing to keep the office of vice-president for its role at the head of the provisional successorship line, whereas the other would abolish the post once its full successorship role was gone, and substitute either the House Speaker or the secretary of state. The group favoring retention of the vice-presidency probably would be disinclined to press for filling a vacated vice-presidency, and although not hostile to reforms attempting to strengthen that office, would be little interested in pursuing that subject. Its priority concern, clearly, would not be matters related to the short-lived acting president but to promoting special presidential elections as the new device to supply full presidents to complete the balance of an interrupted term.[37]

[37] The special election would include the vice-presidency as well, there being no point to permitting the incumbent vice-president to complete his term. However, he would be free, as acting president, to try to secure his party's nomination for either the presidential or the vice-presidential place on the ticket.

Adherents of an alternative view of presidential succession are opposed to special presidential elections, and hence are committed to provision of a satisfactory line of successorship as the preferred mode of filling a vacated presidency. They are impressed, especially in light of the experience of other nations, by the close tie of succession arrangements to the stability of the political order and by the fragility of those arrangements, for they often come into play under conditions of high social stress and tension. A reliance on special elections, involving a constricted caretaker government on the one side and competitive, divisive campaigning on the other, is seen as too great a risk. Better, in this view, to have rapid, automatic, acceptable successorship. Of course, high-quality successors are preferred to mediocre ones, but crisis prevention through orderly office successorship is held to be the number one objective, and if meeting it requires relaxation of standards on the quality of the successor, so be it. Then, too, however deficient the process of vice-presidential selection has been, the nation has comfortably survived past instances of accession to a vacated presidency by the vice-president and, indeed, some of the successors have been judged, at the time and/or in retrospect, to be superior presidents. Therefore, concludes this view, the appropriate direction of solution is to keep and improve the vice-presidency.

The analysis here undertaken has concluded that only marginal changes in the vice-presidency are feasible in the sense of being consistent with a set of key systemic constraints: the vice-president should be of the same party and preferably of the same policy orientation as the president, and the presidential nominee/president should have dominant influence over the designation of his running mate/vice-president. Within these constraints, only limited change is acceptable with respect to retaining an elective vice-presidency. Significantly more time for designating the running mate can be had only by pushing beyond the convention and denying it any direct role in that decision. In exchange, this would increase opportunity for—but not guarantee—more party consultation, more considered review of the alternatives and of the potential nominees' backgrounds, and the like. Still, the decision would remain essentially in the hands of the head of the ticket, and his criteria for choice would not undergo change.

The more novel idea of an appointive vice-presidency would constitute a large change in form, but a markedly lesser one in practice. It would displace the elective vice-presidency and retain the same authority, including primary successorship to a presidency vacated by the elected president. Its legitimacy would be at least equal to if not greater than that of an elective vice-presidency. Under present arrangements, the party convention formally selects the vice-presidential nominee, but the choice is actually made by the freshly nominated head of the ticket. Similarly, the voters' election of a vice-president is more an illusory than a real exercise, because it occurs as a by-product of the electorate's decision on who will be president. With an appointive vice-presidency, legitimacy would rest on nomination by an elected president and confirmation based on a careful review by Congress. Given the populistic temper of the times, however, it probably would be difficult to gain public support for converting the vice-presidency from the elective office it has always been to an appointive one.

Changing to appointed vice-presidents would hold a considerable promise, though not the certainty, of regularly producing presidential successors of presumed good quality. The president, having his election safely behind him, could make his choice with his governing needs uppermost in mind, in contrast to the present situation where the presidential nominee's decision reflects convention commitments or campaign and election needs. The Congress (and the public), though generally disposed to grant the president the nominee of his choice, would expect the designee to be an official of some prominence and repute, one already possessed of a solid record of accomplishment. The likely result would be the selection of vice-presidents generally of a quality superior to the average run of elected vice-presidents, though falling well short of any self-conscious effort to confine the choice to one among those deemed best suited to become president should that office be prematurely vacated. Once in office, however, appointed vice-presidents could not expect to function differently from the characteristic pattern of elected vice-presidents, that is, a presidentially controlled definition of their role and their assignment to significant activities on condition they perform as an agent of the president.

If the concept of an appointive vice-presidency were to be seriously considered for adoption, it should be amended—as should the first two sections of the Twenty-fifth Amendment—to deny to any vice-president appointed by a president other than the elected president the right to succeed to a vacated presidency for the remainder of the term—a successor president, whether he previously was the appointed or the elected vice-president, should not be able to name his immediate full successor. In such circumstances, either contingent succession by the House Speaker or provisional successorship, with a special election, could be used. Although the chances of this type of double vacancy happening are lower than that for a double vacancy under the present system, the latter's recent unanticipated occurrence suggests the wisdom of planning ahead for even remote possibilities.

Such planning and prudence, on this or on other aspects of the presidential succession problem, should be accompanied by humility, because today's solutions to problems of governmental design, as we observed at the beinning of this study, have a way of becoming tomorrow's problems. The reader may take comfort or unease in accepting the likelihood that, whichever option on succession he or she has decided to prefer, it would not work out quite as intended and would necessitate at least a brief return to the drawing board for correction. The illusory pursuit of perfect solutions, which has characterized much of the reform posture on the problem of the vice-presidency and other frustrations of presidential succession, may often appear exhilarating. But as long as we retain the capacity and the freedom to rectify institutional deficiencies on the basis of experience, the search for the best of the imperfect solutions should be no less challenging or satisfying.